MW01292948

My Thirty Years *in* NEW YORK CITY

AN ASPIRING ACTOR'S WANNABE
LIGHTS! CAMERA! ACTION!

JOHN JOSEPH STRANGI

PAGE PUBLISHING, INC.
New York, NY

First originally published by Page Publishing, Inc. 2015

ISBN 978-1-68139-038-3 (pbk)
ISBN 978-1-68139-039-0 (digital)

Printed in the United States of America

For John Castagna

CONTENTS

SEPTEMBER 1972

FAIRY TALES CAN COME TRUE, THEY CAN HAPPEN TO YOU

Well, my lifelong dream has finally come true. I am moving to New York City to be an actor. I cannot believe that the day has finally come. I have waited so long for this dream to become reality. I could barely sleep last night, with all the anticipation of the next day's events. I have a nine o'clock flight in the morning. All my loved ones are with me, at the airport, to wish me good-bye. It's an emotional moment, but I'm too excited to be anything but happy and exuberant. After many kisses and hugs, I am off.

The flight gets off to a nice start. I asked for a window seat where I could have a first-hand look at the grand New York City skyline when we land. I am still bubbling with excitement. I just cannot believe it! Lunchtime arrives and I ask the flight attendant for a cocktail in celebration. I decide on ordering a drink. Wait! Hold it! Something is not right here. John Strangi wants to be an actor? Shy, introverted, Johnny? This just cannot be for real!

Perhaps it is best to begin a few years back. Yes, let us begin with act 1.

ACT 1

A STAR IS BORN

Picture it: Baylor Hospital - Dallas, Texas - September 9, 1953

Mr. and Mrs. Albert Strangi are expecting their fourth child. Albert is a handsome Italian and Genevieve a lovely Irish woman. They have already had one boy and two girls. They are hoping for another boy. The delivery is actually about two weeks early. Genevieve is already a pro at this, but Albert is nervously pacing in the waiting room. Nine a.m. turns into ten a.m. Ten a.m. becomes eleven a.m. Eleven becomes twelve. Albert could stand a nice martini right now, but I digress.

One o'clock arrives and we have struck gold! It is a seven-pound five-ounce baby boy! His name will be John Joseph. The entire family is elated! Is this baby gorgeous or what? Just look at him! Those eyes! That nose! His little feeties! That plump little body! What a beauty! Oh, wait! Oh, wait! This child is yours truly! Fancy that!

After a few days, this new bundle of joy is in his new home. Family and friends are all elated. Little Johnny's act 1 has begun. Did I mention the kid is gorgeous?

The next year goes by rather quickly when Albert and Genevieve decide it would be best to move into a larger house. After much searching, they find the winner in the Mayflower Estates. It is a lovely house in a most impressive neighborhood. Life looks good here for at least the next ten years. Unfortunately, Albert and Genevieve will divorce in 1966 after thirty years of marriage. It was a Lucy and Desi marriage. They loved each other, madly, but it was just not to last. After the divorce, Genevieve will have to be both mother and father to John. Life goes on.

SEPTEMBER 2, 1969

SCHOOL DAYS, SCHOOL DAYS, DEAR OLD GOLDEN RULE DAYS

It is my first day of school. It is high school, at last! I was never a straight A student, *to say the least*, but I did okay in certain subjects. Lunch was my favorite. I was hardly a popular kid, though I did have my select friends. I always thought of myself as a bit shy and introverted, but I tried to rise above it. I even played football my last year of junior high, hoping it might brand me with a bit of "stud status." What good it did! We lost repeatedly and did not even score until the fifth game. It's the thought that counts.

Richardson High School was quite large, though not unlike any other school in the area. After my mother and dad's divorce, we lived in North Dallas but were in the Richardson school district. My senior year, there were close to a thousand kids in my graduating class. That does not leave much elbowroom. My first day of school seemed rather ordinary, until it came to my final class of the day. It was my drama class. The class had about twenty-five students. It was your typical classroom, in the front, a small platform stage for acting.

My lovely teacher, Mrs. Carolyn Doyle, would capture me in her spell instantly. She was gorgeous and had the vivacious personality to go with it. I loved this woman instantly! Wow! What a treasure! We began class by introducing ourselves, one by one, and telling of any interesting experience we had during the summer. Surprisingly, I felt very comfortable being in front of people. I found, as the days went on, being on stage and performing in any way would make me feel totally in control and relaxed. I felt, at last, I had discovered my niche. The name of the school's drama club, which Mrs. Doyle naturally headed, was Playhouse RHS, and once a year, there were auditions. This year's auditions would be at the end of the month. I wanted, so much, to be accepted. For my audition piece, I decided to do a scene from Noel Coward's *Private Lives*. I had always admired Sir Noel's work, and having envied and admired so many British actors through the years, I had developed a jolly good British accent.

The scene I had chosen was between the two husbands, Elliot Chase and Victor Prynne. I would be Elliot, and record the part of Victor on my tape recorder, playing against him. The day arrived for the audition, so I took my spot on the tiny stage and had at it. However, totally in character, I was able to glance at Mrs. Doyle and see that she was pleased with my performance. At least she looked pleased, but one never knows, does one? I did flub up on one line, but I gave my performance an A-.

At the end of the week, during my English class, I received an olive-green envelope. This, apparently, was either my acceptance or refusal into Playhouse. Nervously, I opened the envelope. Alleluia! I was accepted! I felt like I had just won the Oscar. I was thrilled! Being accepted meant the world to me. I then decided I would do everything in my power to advance in the group.

The first play that Playhouse decides to undertake is *Barefoot in the Park*. The roles were almost all given to older students, so I did everything I could do working backstage. I found it so exciting just being a part of it. The smell of greasepaint had me in its power.

The RHS Theater was quite large, as school theaters go, with seating close to one thousand. On opening night, I had the job of climbing up onto the rafters and throwing fake snow at two different times. I was a bit nervous climbing those rickety old rafters, but I tried to rise above it. I did okay, though I did throw the snow down at the wrong time, one of the times. Fortunately, for me, it really did not make too much of a difference, making my "fabulous flub" hardly fatal.

CURTAIN

The next play presented, several months later, was the musical *The King and I*. I tried out for the part of Sir Edward Ramsey and seized it. I was thrilled. It was not a terribly large part, but I loved it. Once again, my British accent came in handy. I made certain that even though I had a part in the show, moving me up a notch, I would still help backstage as much as possible. A Broadway snob, I chose not to be! It was during this musical extravaganza that I realized that Doyle, as we called her now, spared no expense in scenery, costumes, and props, making every high school production look like a Broadway show. We would rent a large quantity of the props and scenery from the Music Hall in downtown Dallas, where the Dallas Summer Musicals reign each year.

THE KING AND I

Act II–Scene I

KING: *I see ladies have not been educated in English custom of spying glass.*

SIR ED: *Oh, my monocle. Was that what frightened them? Hello, Anna, my dear.*

KING: *Who? Who is this arrives unannounced?*

ANNA: *Your majesty, may I present Sir Edward Ramsay?*

LIGHTS, CAMERA, ACTION

Opening night, things could not have gone smoother. I was so excited! It was necessary for me to dress quite formal as my entrance was during the ballroom scene. I would be dancing the waltz with the evening's leading lady, Anna Leonowens. I was a bit nervous, but I was to find out in acting that if one does not get nervous, you are doing something wrong. It so adds to the immense energy of the moment.

The evening was a success! Bravo! I remembered every line and delivered a dynamite performance. Our two leads, Stan Williams and Cynthia Janos, were to deliver outstanding performances as well.

I requested that the cast party be at my house and, happily, the party was very much a success. I must have had about a hundred people over. I enjoyed it immensely. My newfound confidence had made me feel like a male Elsa Maxwell. I've so many friends now and am savoring my new popularity. Bravo!

John Strangi

CURTAIN

At the end of the school year, as was the custom, Playhouse would hold the elections of the offices for the following year. To my immense surprise and utter delight, my fellow classmates elected me vice president. I was truly amazed at the honor. I swear, having the prospect of having such a position never even crossed my mind. Truthfully, I have never been much of a leader, but I will do my best to make things proceed with excellence. Kaki Riblet, a senior and superb actress, would be president.

CURTAIN

A junior finally, and I am so excited about having another year with Doyle. Our first play of the year was *Wait Until Dark*, a drama involving a blind girl with a heroin-filled doll in her possession. Audition time! I landed the part of Sergeant Carlino, a crooked police sergeant/detective newly released from jail.

WAIT UNTIL DARK

CARLINO: *You always had the luck. Some jail they sent you to!*

MIKE: *Didn't they teach you a trade inside?*

CARLINO: *Oh sure…L and L four hours a day.*

MIKE: *L and L?*

CARLINO: *Laundry and latrines. I'm the new Mr. Clean.*

I think Sir Edward Ramsey would be quite aghast at my change of character! Happily, my roles seemed to be getting much larger and with many more lines. I will not need my British accent for this one. The show was set for early November. Kaki Riblet will land the starring role of Suzy Hendrix, the blind girl. My good friend, Michele St. John, would land the part of Gloria, the little girl. Her audition for the role

John Strangi

was dynamite! I thought she was great. Doyle asked me if I would shave my sideburns, my current look, for the show, but I refused. I loved those babies! Hell, I think I was shaving when I was eleven. It must be the Italian in me.

November arrives and it's showtime. The bulk of the play takes place in Suzy Hendrix's Greenwich Village apartment. The play went extremely well both nights. I'm thrilled that I am showing my vast versatility as a performer. I thought I, as well as the rest of the cast, was super. I love being on stage more and more. This just has to be my life's work! I feel like I come alive when I go onstage. Perhaps I am being a bit too dramatic. What must be must be.

CURTAIN

Now we are talking major dreams coming true! For years, I had hoped of one day having the opportunity of playing Henry Higgins in *My Fair Lady*. I always loved that show, not to mention its divine Julie Andrews. I think I had been in love with her ever since *Mary Poppins* (I would say this to her in person years later). As fate would have it, Doyle chose *Lady* to be our musical. Now I never thought of myself as the best singer in the world, but since I can sort of talk/sing the songs, like Rex Harrison, this should work. The day of the audition arrives. Things could not have gone smoother! That role was tailor-made for me. When I sang "I've Grown Accustomed to Her Face," Doyle cried. I am Henry Higgins! The part is mine! My singing was a success. I am elated. My good friend, Sharon Worthington, landed the part of Eliza. She has a lovely singing voice. The part of Eliza has so many dimensions to it. All of which she captured beautifully.

Look at her, a prisoner of the gutters.

MY FAIR LADY

HIGGINS: *Eliza! Have some chocolates.*

ELIZA: *How do I know what might be in them. I've heard of girls being drugged by the like of you.*

HIGGINS: *Pledge of good faith, Eliza. I eat one-half and you eat the other. You shall have boxes of them, barrels of them, every day. You shall live on them, eh?*

ELIZA: *I wouldn't have ate it, only I'm too ladylike to take it out of me mouth.*

Condemned by every syllable she utters.

There will be two evening performances. Rehearsals began immediately. What a large cast! They could make up a small city! This was going to be no easy project, but what a challenge! What an adventure! I have so many lines to learn! The stage directions and complicated blocking were endless! The many, many rehearsals to make things picture perfect was without end!

John Strangi & Company

Day by day, things begin to shape up beautifully. The sets and costumes are all gorgeous! They are all worthy of a Broadway opening. Our dancers and choreography are all first rate. Bob Fosse would have approved. Things were going smoothly and made to order when the day before opening I literally lost my voice. I could not speak. All my hard work and constant vocalizing had taken its toll. "Oh dear God, let there be a miracle." Well, there was a miracle. For the next day, opening, my voice was back.

It is showtime! I am counting the minutes until my dream comes true. Eight o'clock arrives! The auditorium goes black! Overture! Curtain up! Opening night goes smoothly without a glitch. From my opening acts "Why Can't the English" to its final "I've Grown Accustomed to Her Face," all went picture perfect. I remember crying at the end. I don't know if it was my character crying or just me out of my pure happiness.

By right she should be taken out and hung.

The second night was to go just as well with the exception of one minor mistake. "The Rain in Spain" sequence involves three different small scenes. At the beginning of each, the prop girl hands a different prop to me, the prop reminding me which scene is taking place. Mistakenly, an ice pack, the third scenes prop, is given to me at the start of the second scene. I immediately begin the dialogue of the third scene. I catch a glimpse of the orchestra conductor, hysterically flipping through the pages of the sheet music and catch my mistake. His cue was all wrong. Realizing my error, I flop my ice pack onto my costar Pickering's head saying "Oh, here you are" and proceed with the proper dialogue of the second scene. My ice pack adlib did get a laugh at least. It was another perfect evening. Another dream comes true!

I let someone else throw the cast party this time. (I was exhausted!)

For the coldblooded murder of the English tongue.

MORNING AFTER

I wake up around nine o'clock in the morning still feeling high from the evening's festivities. I go outside to get the morning paper. Accidentally, I shut the front door. I am locked out of the house and remember that Mother had taken the car to the store. So what am I to do? I remember that one of the windows to the front bedroom is half-broken. This is no problem! I will just remove the half window-pane and slip through the window. As I grasp the broken pane, it quickly slides off, slashing my underarm. I get through the window with blood pouring out of my arm. I do my best to stop the bleeding, but with its force, my best is not the best. At this moment, Mother returns, and seeing the bloody mess, she screams. At which point, after all the blood loss, I pass out. I come to after a few minutes. We then drive to the hospital where I get thirty stitches.

What a nightmare! Less than twenty-four hours ago, I was in seventh heaven and look where I am now, in a hospital room, lying down, staring up at a filthy ceiling and with a bandaged arm. This just cannot be real! Only it is. We drive home and try as best we can to get control of our nerves. I take it easy the rest of the day. I am still in a state of disbelief and hope that I will wake from this nightmare very soon. No such luck. Reality sucks!

Unfortunately, and most disturbingly, this experience will seem to set a certain constant pattern in my life. Whenever anything truly special and outstanding happens to me, it always seems to be followed by some major catastrophe.

Monday arrives and it is back to school. There were many, many compliments of my Henry Higgins. I more than welcomed them. Everyone was a bit shocked to see my arm in a sling and some kidded that my performance was not that bad. "Very funny!"

I remember one teacher asking me if I had seen the show. Am I a good actor or what! He did not even realize that I was Higgins.

CURTAIN

It is the end of the school year and it is time to elect new officers of Playhouse. Everyone assumes that I will be elected president, myself included, thank you very much! The elections are to be around five o'clock at the end of the day. As I walk down the hall to the classroom, friend after friend whispers to me, "John, you have got it in the bag. The presidency is yours!" All want to celebrate after.

One by one, the classroom fills. Kaki takes her position at the podium. I take my position directly behind her. After the usual reading of the minutes, it is time for the announcement of elections for next year's officers. President, vice president, and secretary-treasurer are up for grabs. The president position will be first. It is believed to be between me and my good friend, Michele St. John. Ballots passed out! Beads of sweat gather on my forehead. I hear Kaki whisper on the side, "Oh, please let it be Michele." I hold my tongue. The ballots counted! I lost the position by one vote. I was shattered! I was, literally, almost in tears. Actually, I think I was in tears, but I gathered my composure enough to congratulate Michele. I try to think positive. "With all the starring roles I'm bound to have next year, what time would I have devoting time to president anyway."

Now it is time to elect vice president. Well, now I know I will get vice president again, at the very least. I mean, this just has to be! Once again, ballots are distributed. My sweaty torso now joins those beads of perspiration on my forehead. My back feels drenched. Okay, I admit it! I am not good under pressure. The votes are in. Drum roll, please. I lost by one vote! Just shoot me! This cannot be for real! Only it is. I am crushed! Real men don't cry, or do they?

The election of secretary/treasurer is next. Okay, if I don't get this, I'm booking a passage to Ellis Island. Ballots handed out! Votes tallied! I won by a landslide. Big deal! Was this a demotion or what! I must be positive! I must get ahold of myself! What free time will I have to devote to a silly position anyway?

CURTAIN

It's my last year of high school. I'm a senior at last. Wow! This is cool! One more year and it's time for an entire new chapter. *"The hills are alive."*

The first play that Doyle chooses for us is Neil Simon's *Plaza Suite*. It's a wonderful play taking place in New York City's charming Plaza Hotel. It is, basically, three miniplays in one. The third miniplay is the funniest of the three, and is the one that Michele and I prepare to audition. The first one is the most serious of the three, involving a middle-aged love affair. Different actors are to perform each miniplay.

The day of the audition arrives. Doyle has me read for all three miniplays. She whispers to me that I read well enough to play all three. However, as it turned out, I was the only one who read the first miniplay the best, so that was the role I got. That's cool! At least I'm in it. Michele did land the female lead in the third play that we had rehearsed. Another good friend of mine, Lyn Breeland, will star opposite Michele. He's a good actor and quite the comedian.

PLAZA SUITE

SAM: No, I'm not having an affair with her.

KAREN: Yes, you are.

SAM: Curses, trapped again. It looks like snow. I hope I can get a cab.

KAREN: Even if you're not Sam, it's alright if you do.
I approve of Miss McCormack.

Rehearsals seemed to be going well the next couple of weeks. We tried to make our set look as much like the Plaza Hotel's suite as much as possible. I suggested they use a lovely white sofa that is in my mother's bedroom. We hired a truck immediately and made the switch. The sofa looked super. It fit in with the stage setting, beautifully. If nothing else, I'll feel at home.

SHOWTIME

Opening night of *Plaza Suite* turned out to be a bit hectic. My opening act/scene couldn't have gone better. The girl, Julie Hawkins, who played my wife, was brilliant! I loved working with her. To quote our newspaper review the following day: "John Strangi's performance was to be expected, but Julie Hawkins was a pleasant surprise." The third miniplay went smoothly as well. The problem was with the second one. Its male lead, Stuart Murchison, had not learned his lines too well, causing the female lead, Debra Duggan, to become quite annoyed and frantic, to say the least. After their performance, she was using four-letter words even I had never heard of. I accompanied Debra, afterward, to a nearby bar to try to calm her down, but no words could really save the evening. There was no real cast party due to the jumbled mess.

THERE'S NO BUSINESS LIKE SHOW BUSINESS

A few weeks later, during the weekend, I noticed an ad in the newspaper for open auditions at a Theater Three, a relatively new professional theater near downtown Dallas. Therefore, off I go to audition for their play *The Play's the Thing*, being directed by a Larry O'Dwyer, who was also a gifted actor in the Dallas area. I tried out for the part of Mel, the male social secretary, and I got it. I was so excited! I could not believe it. I was going to be in my first professional show! My cup runneth over.

The next month's rehearsals would be almost every evening. I thought the play was coming along pretty well. The play consisted of three acts, and I did not make my entrance until the third act. I liked our director, Mr. O'Dwyer, at first, but with each evening found working with him a bit more challenging. The show must go on! The play will last two months.

Opening night went without a hitch. I was pleased with my performance. I never smoked cigarettes my entire life, but I smoked during the entire run of this show. I wasn't smoking onstage, but smoking offstage. It was nerve-racking each evening having to wait until the third act to make my entrance, so I puffed and puffed until my entrance. Perhaps a martini might have worked better. The reviews in the papers were mixed, but not bad. At least they spelled my name right. We did play for close to two months with relatively full houses.

The next play, to be presented by Theater Three, was to be the musical *The Venetian Twins*. Jac Alder, cofounder of the theater, was to direct. I auditioned for the role of Lelio and I got it. It was a challenge, for every night I sang several songs, solo, and had to have three sword fights. Of my three sword fights, two of them were with none other than Larry O'Dwyer, who was starring in the show. Oops!

John Strangi

Larry O'Dwyer was a brilliant actor, but I remember a few of the evenings I felt like we were really going at it during the sword fights, unscripted. Unfortunately, my role, Lelio, was instructed to lose every sword fight. Now that I am a *tad* older, I find it best to make every effort to get along with one's fellow actors, but during this show, Larry's and my relationship suffered greatly from artistic differences. Nonetheless, I am happy to say, *The Venetian Twins* received excellent reviews in all the papers. Bravo!

With all my time devoted to Theater Three, I wasn't able to appear in many of my school's productions, with the exception of *The Serpent* where I played God.

My senior year was ending, and it was time to decide on the next year's agenda. After much research, I decided that the two best drama schools in New York City were the American Academy of Dramatic Arts and Julliard. Julliard was my first choice.

As fate would have it, Julliard was scheduling auditions in Dallas for April. I immediately submitted the fifty-dollar audition fee and scheduled the audition. What was even more unbelievable was that the auditions were being conducted at Theater Three, during the run of *The Venetian Twins*. I couldn't believe it. Is this fate or what? It's meant to be! On top of that, the man holding the auditions is Mr. John Houseman. There is a theater in New York City named after him for God's sake!

After checking through a number of monologues for my audition, I decide on performing a piece from *Look Back in Anger*. Don't ask me why, but I remember distinctly that I didn't even bother reading the entire play. Was that stupid or what? It goes without saying that not reading the entire play is a major no-no. One has to read the entire play to capture the true essence of one's character, but I did not do it. Actually, with me being so full of confidence these days, I just did not think it was necessary. I'm sure I'll knock 'em dead!

Big mistake! Major blunder! Do not pass go! Do not collect a hundred dollars!

The day of the audition arrives and I nervously prepare for my performance. Reluctantly, after a million second thoughts, I decide to bring my scrapbook along with me so I can show Mr. Houseman all my many theatrical accomplishments. Does this look unprofessional or what! I was not of the opinion then, but now such behavior seems very amateurish. After a shy compliment or two from Mr. Houseman, it is time to perform.

It's a funny thing that even though I have been working in this theater and on this stage for weeks, performing in front of Mr. Houseman made it feel like my very first time there. I think, sadly, my audition performance proved it. I performed mediocre at best. I knew this the second that I stumbled through my final line.

Mr. Houseman, naturally, was the perfect gentleman. Being most familiar with *Look Back in Anger*, he quickly dissected my performance, explaining how I had hardly portrayed my character properly. Sadly, I knew his critique was on target. I repeat, "If I had only read the play!" It's moments like this that I have no choice but to resort to a Mary Poppins outlook and hope for the best. Hell, perhaps he will sense my immense talent, looking beyond my performance. I can only hope. "Just a spoonful of sugar helps the medicine go down." Bring on the sugar! Please!

A very slow month goes by and I hurry to our mailbox to find the letter from Julliard. Excitedly, I open the envelope. "Oh please, oh please, let it be an acceptance!" You guessed it. It is a rejection. I am crushed. "Damn! Damn! Damn! Damn!" Okay. I must get control. I will not let this get me down, however disappointed I am.

The following week my ego received a bit of a lift. I received a letter in the mail requesting that I, as well as some of the other top drama students in Dallas, attend the Dallas movie premiere of the new movie *Junior Bonner*, starring Steve McQueen and Ida Lupino. My best friend Michele was asked as well.

The day of the premiere arrives and we are off to the theater in a bus. Surprisingly, Ms. Lupino would be a passenger on the bus. We all, naturally, met her. She was charming. At the theater, I also met her costar Ben Johnson. Mr. Johnson was just recently awarded an Oscar for his work in *The Last Picture Show*. I asked him what it was like holding an Oscar, for which he replied, "My hands are still numb." He seemed very personable and down to earth. *Bonner* also starred Robert Preston, so it was certainly not lacking its named performers. As far as movies go, though, it was really nothing to write home about. It just didn't work.

Speaking of work, it's time for me to get back to work, work being to find my New York acting school. Enter the American Academy of Dramatic Arts!

CURTAIN

I ask my mother if it would be okay if I fly to New York for an audition with the American Academy of Dramatic Arts. My mom, who has always been more than supportive, says yes. I, excitedly, call the academy and arrange the audition. I am thrilled! My audition will be on Friday and I will do a monologue from *My Fair Lady*. God knows I read that play! All is set! She even agreed on my spending an entire week there, where I could really absorb the city's magic. Aren't mothers wonderful!

JUNE 1972

MY WEEK IN NEW YORK CITY

It is a beautiful Tuesday morning. I wake up feeling refreshed, though I did have a bit of trouble sleeping. The anticipation and excitement of my soon to be NYC journey was dominating my brain. After a quick shave and shower, I head to the kitchen and devour my breakfast in record time. I call a cab to deliver me to the airport. I gather my gear, kiss my mother good-bye, and am off.

My cab arrives at the airport about 9:00 a.m., giving me plenty of time for my 11:30 a.m. flight. I always prefer getting to the airport major early, giving me plenty of time to spare. One never knows the amount of people and what long lines to expect. Fortunately, the lines at the ticket counter are minimal and my bags checked in no time. I head for my gate and patiently wait for the plane. Boarding begins about ten forty-five. I request a window seat where I can be the first to catch a glimpse of New York's breathtaking skyline. With time to kill before my flight, I head to the newspaper stand to buy a magazine or two and perhaps a book of crossword puzzles. On the way back to the gate, I also grab a cup of coffee and a doughnut. I sit and start a crossword puzzle or two hoping to make the time fly fast. Ten forty-five arrives! "Now boarding flight 18 to New York City's LaGuardia." I cannot believe it! Oh yes! Oh yes! Oh yes! It's up, up, and away!

I get in the line to board and proceed to my window seat, which was pretty much in the middle of the plane. I ain't first-class yet, "but just watch out, world!" The flight takes off smoothly, and after about twenty minutes, the flight attendant asks if I would care for a drink. I decide to order a "Manhattan," a drink I had never had before. It only seemed fitting to order one. She hands me the drink, and I immediately take a gulp. I hate it! It just is not my cup of tea. A vodka man I be! I finish it anyway. A stale lunch follows, but it does not matter. I am on my way to the Big Apple! The hours fly by quicker than I had hoped and we approach the city. I could not wait to set my eyes upon that beautiful New York skyline! Wow! It is all too gorgeous for words.

We land. I depart the plane, gather my bags, hail a cab, and it is off to the hotel. I chose a hotel on Fifty-Seventh Street where I would be in close range of the theater district. I check in, go to my room, throw my bags on the bed, and set out for the city, walking toward Times Square. I feel like today is Christmas! Wow! You can feel the energy! It's magical! There is just nothing like it in the world! The neon lights! The immense billboards! The theaters! The towering buildings! The golden hustle and bustle of people! I love it! I love it! I love it! It is a bit of a walk but I decide to venture to Thirty-Eighth Street and Madison where the American Academy of Dramatic Arts is. My audition is not until Friday, but I'd just like to see it.

I make it to AADA. A small group of steps leads to its front door. You can tell that it has been around awhile, but it's lovely. I say hello to the woman at the reception desk and tell her of my coming audition. She wishes me good luck. On the wall is a large picture of many of their successful graduates. I am overcome with excitement!

I head on back to the hotel. I decide to go up Fifth Avenue where I can pass Tiffany's, Saks, Bergdorf Goodman—all the great stores. Going across Fifty-Seventh Street, I walk by the Russian Tea Room and Carnegie Hall. I am in awe of everything.

Before going up to my room, I decide to visit the Broadway Tickets desk and purchase at least some of my tickets for the week's shows. I want to see a show every evening. I buy tickets for the first four evenings: *No No Nannette*, *Follies*, *Butterflies Are Free*, and *Ain't Supposed to Die a Natural Death*. Am I over-dosing a bit too much on musicals? Gloria Swanson is starring in *Butterflies*. Just to think that I will get to see a legend like her in person! All the shows have legends. *Follies* overflows with them.

Nighttime arrives and I prepare for *Nannette*. I decide to have a drink at Sardi's before the show, so

I leave the hotel at around six thirty. I adore Sardi's with the many, many star caricatures on its walls. You can feel the energy in the room. Who knows, but maybe one day my picture will grace one of its walls. All these pictures on the walls are just fascinating. They must go back to the twenties! I sense that Sardi's will turn out to be one of my favorite hangouts. When I can afford it, that is.

Nannette is playing at the Forty-Sixth Street Theater, and Sardi's is on Forty-Fourth Street. I decide to leave at seven thirty for the theater anyway. I do not want to be a minute late. I must hear that overture. I arrive at the theater, find my seat, and prepare for ecstasy. The overture begins, sending chills through my body. It always has. Curtain up! The costumes, the scenery, the music, the dancing—everything is perfection! Helen Gallagher, its principal female lead, is exceptional. Her dancing is priceless! Bobby Van is remarkable as well. What a thrill to see the legend, Ruby Keeler, too. Somebody pinch me.

After the show, I decide to have dinner at Sardi's. I am already feeling like it is a second home. "I'll drink to that!" I head back to the hotel around eleven thirty. What an evening! Please do not let this magical dream ever end.

WEDNESDAY

I LIKE NEW YORK IN JUNE

Good morning, New York! It's another gorgeous day in the Big Apple.

First on my morning agenda is buying show tickets for my final two days. I know now how quickly shows sell out. I head to the tickets counter to purchase them. I am needing a Saturday and a Sunday show. What shall I choose? What shall I pick? For my final two shows, I decide on *Applause,* starring Anne Baxter, and *Oh Calcutta. Oh Calcutta* is the new musical where the entire cast is in their birthday suits. Oh my! Oh my! Oh my! Very interesting!

I spent the day roaming the streets, cherishing every single precious moment. I walked my legs off today, seeing as much of the city as possible. The Plaza Hotel is gorgeous! I forced myself to have a Bloody Mary at their Oak Bar. Their Oak Bar is so beautiful with its many large murals of spectacular landscape and such. What a beauty! I must have roamed through every great department store: Saks! Bergdorf Goodman! Tiffany's! Lord & Taylor! Each one is more spectacular than the other!

This evening is *Butterflies Are Free* with Gloria Swanson at the Booth on Forty-Fifth Street. I would have loved seeing *Butterflies* with its original cast starring Eileen Heckart. I have loved Ms. Heckart's priceless acting all of my life! She was such a legend. I was thrilled when she won the Oscar for *Butterflies* the movie. I felt like I had won. Her performance was golden!

I got to the theater about seven thirty, like last night. There was no overture this time, but I still got the chills when they raised the curtain. I loved the show and thought Ms. Swanson was brilliant! It is so exciting to see a legend like her! After the show I just grabbed a small bite to eat at a nearby Italian restaurant that I thought looked inviting, which it was. I am feeling more like a New Yorker every day.

THURSDAY

I'M IN A NEW YORK STATE OF MIND

Today, I thought I would venture to Greenwich Village and get a taste of Lower Manhattan. I took a subway there and got off at Fourteenth Street. The Village was charming. I tried to see as much of it as possible. Many of their streets were still with their old-world cobblestone. I found Bleecker and MacDougal streets lovely. To think of the years and years they have been around. Washington Square was also a looker.

This evening was my date with *Follies*, the new big Stephen Sondheim musical. It was playing at the Winter Garden theatre off Fiftieth. What a cast in this one! It stars Alexis Smith, Dorothy

Collins, and Yvonne De Carlo, just to mention a few. I did my bit at Sardi's first. Certain things one must do! After a dynamite martini, I headed to the theater. I got there just before eight, still with plenty of time to hear that golden overture. It was golden! What a score! What scenery! What choreography! Every single actor was perfection! It was just beautiful! I loved it!

After, while at Sardi's, a fellow mentioned to me of another "theatrical restaurant bar" that is a hangout for many employed and  unemployed actors called Joe Allen's. I thought I would give it a try, which I did. It was on Forty-Seventh Street between Seventh and Eighth Avenues. I loved it! I sat at the bar and then grabbed a table for a bite to eat. It was interesting that all of the pictures on the walls were of Broadway shows that had all flopped. What a novel idea! I met so many colorful and dynamic actors there.

FRIDAY

GIVE MY REGARDS TO BROADWAY

Well, today is the day! My audition for AADA is at one o clock. At last the day has come! I order room service, having only a light breakfast of coffee and bagel with cream cheese. Anything heavier might interfere with all the butterflies in my stomach. After gobbling it down, I hop in the shower, shave, and attack my day's itinerary. I then decide, naturally, to practice my *My Fair Lady* monologue. I can recite the entire play backward, but practice makes perfect. I've chosen to perform Higgins's *I'm An Ordinary Man*. Although it is primarily a song, I will be speaking it, reciting it with a British accent. I hope that is not a mistake. I could always Americanize it if they like. I just think it sounds so good, British, and after all, it is from *My Fair Lady*. They will love it either way! How could they not! I will wear a pair of gray slacks, yellow shirt, and blue blazer. I consider wearing a tie but chose not to. I want to feel more relaxed. I check myself out

in the mirror again and again and again and again. "Enough already, you look great!"

 I decide to take a cab to the audition, fear that the walk there might leave me a bit ruffled. I have to look my best! My cab drops me off at twelve forty-five. I walk up the tiny staircase to the entrance, tell the receptionist I have arrived, and then is led to the room where my audition is to take place. I am solo at present. No one else is in the room. It is a rather large room with a large rectangular desk on the side. I am guessing that is where my judges will be sitting. Right, I am! For at one o'clock exactly they arrive. My judges consist of two women and two gentlemen. (At least I hope they are gentle.) We exchange greetings and have at it.

"I find the moment that a woman makes friends with me, she becomes jealous, exacting, suspicious, and a damn nuisance." I recite line after line, without a hitch, and feeling very good about my performance. I just hope they do too. They ask me to wait outside for a moment then about fifteen minutes later invite me back in. They greet me with the colossal news that *I was accepted!* I am overcome with joy. I just cannot believe it! I felt like kissing them all! Wow! This is beyond cool! This is just too much!

I leave the academy practically skipping all the way back to the hotel. I cannot get the smile off my face, nor do I want to. I just feel like I have never felt before! I reach the hotel, running up to my room, to call Mother and tell her. She is so happy for me! She knows how much it means to me. I then call my brother, Albert, to tell him. He is equally ecstatic. I just do not know when I have been happier.

This evening's show is *Ain't Supposed to Die a Natural Death*. It's playing at the Ambassador Theater on Forty-Ninth Street. It's an all-black musical, centering on ghetto life, I believe. As usual, I head over to Sardi's at about six thirty. This time I go to the bar on the second floor. It is just as nice and crowded as the one on the first floor. I must have told everyone of my acceptance into the academy, even the coat check girl. I think I like the second floor bar even better than the first floor. I am standing next to some lovely women from London. It is fate! I share with them my AADA victory as Henry

Higgins. They ask to hear me recite a bit of my audition piece. I willingly oblige. They tell me my accent is perfection! The bartender seems to enjoy my performance as well. In fact, the entire second floor bar gave me a round of applause. "No autographs, please!" I finish my martini and head to the theater wishing them "cheerio."

AIN'T ain't the best musical I ever saw, but it was okay. All of the actors were very talented, and their singing and dancing were first rate. I think I just prefer my shows to have more of a happy theme. I decide to go to Joe Allen's after the show. It was packed, but I managed to get a seat at the bar. Into the evening, two very theatrical-looking fellows sat next to me at the bar. It turned out that they were two of the dancers in *Follies*. What a thrill meeting them! I could not compliment them enough and went on and on about how much I loved the show. They were both charming and wished me all the luck in the world with my new theatrical endeavor. I felt, at Joe Allen's, it was one big happy family. They are mostly all actors and all trying to hold on to that brass ring.

I take a cab back to the hotel. Many calls and voice mails are waiting for me. They were all congratulations from family and friends. News certainly travel fast!

SATURDAY

I HAPPEN TO LIKE NEW YORK

It is another lovely day in New York. I never sleep late, as a rule, but this morning I didn't wake up till almost eleven. Maybe it was that glorious dream I had, my acceptance into the American Academy of Dramatic Arts. Oops! That wasn't a dream, was it! Nice! Once again, I order breakfast to the room, a pot of coffee and a few Danish.

What shall I do today? I have it! I think a nice brunch at the Plaza Hotel in their Palm Court would suit me fine. Oh yes! Oh yes! Oh yes! Let's do it. After a quick shower and shave, I am on my way. As my hotel is on Fifty-Seventh Street and the Plaza is on Fifty-Ninth,

I will just walk. I just have to go further east. I put on my blue blazer and I am off. The Plaza is so gorgeous! They just do not make them like this anymore. I had a nice brunch, accompanied by my beloved Bloody Mary. That Bloody Mary is getting to be as common as Sardi's.

On the way back to the hotel, I pay another visit to Tiffany's. I mean, it is right there on Fifty-Seventh Street. Why the hell not! What a gorgeous store. Just think of all the gifted and brilliant people who have passed through that door. Needless to say, I cannot really afford much to buy right now, but my day shall come! Mark my word! I also pay another quick visit to Bergdorf Goodman on Fifty-Seventh Street. What a gorgeous store! Their windows could be mini-Broadway shows. Brilliant! Actually, I take my time, walking, exploring many of the smaller shops on the cross streets. I find them all charming. I arrive back to the hotel around five o'clock and take a short rest before the evening's festivities.

The show tonight will be *Oh Calcutta*. It's that musical where the cast bares it all. It should be an eye-opener, to say the least. After the show, I thought I would try a Mama Leone's, an Italian restaurant I had run across in one of my Playbills. It might be a bit of a tourist trap, but "when in Rome."

It is off to Sardi's at six tonight. I grab my stool at the upstairs bar again. It seems even busier tonight, with it being Saturday. Just as I reach the end of the staircase, who do I see at a nearby table, but Maureen Stapleton, with three friends. Well, I just have to say something to her. I have always admired her work so much. After about thirty minutes, with my martini, I gather my courage to say something to Ms. Stapleton. I nervously approach her table and simply say, "Ms. Stapleton, I hope I'm not disturbing you, but I just had to thank you and tell you how much I have admired your work through the years." She thanked me and I went back to my stool. Strangely enough, she seemed a bit more nervous than I did. Maybe she read my reviews in *Lady*. Yeah, right! It is showtime and it is off to the theater. My seat was center orchestra. It is easier to get great seats when one is alone.

Oh Calcutta did turn out to be an eye-opener. I would hardly say there was any great plot, but who is looking for a plot with sixty naked bodies parading in front of you? I can appreciate eyeing Adonis-like figures, but many of the parading figures on the stage hardly fell into that category. Well, all I can say is if I attempt to get a part in *this* show, I have got to lose ten pounds, and it's best my diet begins after Mama Leone's.

Mama Leone's was okay though it seemed like a bit of a circus. So much is crowded in New York, but this restaurant seemed major crowded. Its decor was that of a major gondola. Their lasagna was fine, but I doubt Julia Child would give them four stars. Still, it is another New York moment.

SUNDAY

THE COSTUMES, THE SCENERY, THE MAKEUP, THE PROPS

It's another lovely day in New York. I wake up around seven and order breakfast. Then it is a quick shave and shower. This will be my last full day, for my plane back to Dallas leaves at five tomorrow.

My show today is a one o'clock matinee. I cannot wait to see *Applause*. I could not have picked a better show to end my trip with, its theme being the theater and all its trappings. It now stars Ann Baxter who played Eve Harrington in the movie. I would have loved to have seen it, with its original star, Lauren Bacall, but I'm sure Ms. Baxter will be great. It is playing at the Palace.

 Even though I have tickets for an early show, I still venture out for some more exploring. I head to the east side today. I first visit Grand Central Station. I cannot believe that I had not gone there yet, but with so much in New York to see, it is understandable. What an immense spectacle it is! Wow! It is gorgeous! I then wander up and down Second and Third Avenues. There are so many lovely little shops. When noon approaches, I grab a bite to eat at the Oyster Bar in Grand Central and head on back. I go up to my room and rest a bit before my final show. How it hurts to have to say that!

I arrive to the theater about twelve thirty for the one o'clock show. The theater is packed, and once again, my center orchestra seat is exceptional. Lights out! Overture! Curtain up! You can feel the excitement in the room.

Applause at the Tony Awards had won best musical along with Lauren Bacall. I certainly can tell why. What a hit! Every second is golden. It makes me cry. The singing and dancing are all the best! Everything is picture perfect. Needless to say, the show represents the life I hope to have. Ms. Baxter's performance, along with the rest of the cast, is superb!

After the show, I walk up to Fifty-Ninth Street, deciding to have an afternoon cocktail in the Oak Bar at the Plaza. I am getting to be friends with the bartenders there as well. I sat at the bar while playing repeatedly in my head the many visions of the glorious show I had just seen. After my drink, I walk over to the west side and wander around there a bit.

A woman at the front desk, at my hotel, had told me of a lovely restaurant on the west side called Café des Artistes. She said it had been there since 1917 and that I would love it. Naturally, it is too early for dinner, but I thought I would look anyway. I walked to Sixty-Seventh Street to find it. I loved it! It is just beautiful. It has a European look to it with many large, picturesque murals. I made an eight thirty dinner reservation for that evening. It is back to the hotel for a wee rest before dinner. I decide to write a few more postcards to the people I forgot to write. Granted, I will get there before the postcards but it is the thought that counts.

Dinnertime approaches and I decide to take a cab to Café des Artiste's. I arrive there about eight fifteen and escorted to my table even though I am a bit early. This café transmits that wonderful feeling of a nightclub from the 1920s. I feel like I am in Paris! After my token martini, I order dinner of filet mignon with béarnaise. It was delicious! I am so happy to have discovered this gem of a restaurant.

I take a cab back to the hotel around eleven. I am sad when I realize that this is my last time of hitting the pillow in this glorious city.

MONDAY

SO LONG! FAREWELL! ALVEDERZANE! GOOD-BYE!

All good things must come to an end, I guess. That is not to say you cannot make them reappear, however, which is exactly what I intend to do! Mark my word!

I woke up this morning around six thirty. I want to have as much of my last day as possible. I take a quick shower and shave, and go downstairs for a small breakfast. After breakfast, I go to the front desk and ask them if I could check my bags with them after my one o'clock checkout. They, of course, said yes and that it would be no problem at all. My flight back to Dallas is scheduled to leave at 5:00 p.m.

I set out for the east-side crowd, deciding to spend my last "NYC am" with them. As far as living here goes, I think I would prefer being on the east side. Both east and west are great; however, I am leaning more toward the east. I walk across Fifty-Seventh Street to First Avenue and Sutton Place down to Beekman Place. I walk past 17 Beekman where Irving Berlin lived for so many years. What a gorgeous townhouse he owned, and what a legend he was. I had heard that Turtle Bay is crawling with celebrities, Stephen Sondheim and Katharine Hepburn among them. (Years later I will meet Kate and Stephen and set foot in both their townhouses.) Turtle Bay is lovely. Katharine Hepburn has owned a townhouse there since the late twenties. Talk about a good investment! Afternoon approaches! I grab a light lunch and sadly head back to the hotel to collect my bags. What must be must be.

I hail a cab, arrive at La Guardia about three, check my bags, and head for my gate. I board at four thirty and take my seat. I think of the outstanding and colossal time I just had. What a week! I have so many beautiful memories. My plane lands around 7:30 p.m. I collect my bags, grab a cab, and it is back to reality. Reality stinks!

FAST-FORWARD A MONTH

It is a sunny day in Big D. The phone rings a little after 10:00 a.m. It is my brother, Albert. He tells me that Dad would like to see me this afternoon. I wonder why. Afternoon approaches and I get to Dad's house around one thirty. After a hug and kiss or two with him and his wife, he asks me to join him in his office. I am thinking and hoping that it is just to discuss my New York plans like my allowance, my lodging, and all the financials involved. Well, I was right. He did want to discuss New York. He asked me to can the idea of going to New York and agree to attend a four-year college in Texas. Just shoot me! I was close to tears and crushed. He was never a supporter of my acting. Never! All my hopes and dreams are gone! To my immense surprise, after a couple of hours of my begging and pleading with him, I did get him to change his mind. You see how one's acting will come in handy. "Happy days are here again."

So begins…

MY THIRTY YEARS IN NYC

Where we left off…

SEPTEMBER 1972

FAIRY TALES CAN COME TRUE, THEY CAN HAPPEN TO YOU

Midflight, I order a drink from the flight attendant. This time it will not be a Manhattan, but I must have a celebratory cocktail. I decide on champagne.

Champagne in hand, I ponder what an exciting year I have waiting for me. New York City! Drama school! Theater! Broadway! I am feeling those chills that run through me when I hear that overture at the beginning of a show. It is a smooth flight and, after three glasses of champagne, seems even smoother. We approach NYC, and once again, I see that tremendous skyline. There is just nothing in the world like it. School does not begin for a week, so I will be staying at a hotel until I find new lodging.

The plane makes a smooth landing. I hurry to baggage, claim my bags, and quickly hail a cab to the city. It is not a smooth cab ride to the hotel. I am soon to discover that a cab ride is rarely smooth in New York City. Cabbies do not drive. They fly. Their reckless behavior will soon become second nature to me. I am dropped off at my hotel and shown to my room. I unpack, change clothes, and then head outside. I still cannot believe I am really here! I roam around everywhere: East! West! North! South! Uptown! Downtown! I almost have to pinch myself to believe it is all for real.

With this being my first day, I decide to put off my apartment searching until tomorrow. Maybe I will just have drinks and dinner at good old Sardi's tonight and tell the gang I am back! At six thirty, I do just that. I decide to do the downstairs bar. First tonight, though, I would not forget to tell the bartenders upstairs hello as well. Most of the bartenders have worked there for years and years. Just imagine the many great stories they could tell. I am sure they have rubbed elbows with the best. I sit down for dinner at about nine and then head over to Joe Allen's after ten. I have to tell the gang there as well that I am back. It is great seeing them all! I feel like they are family. One of the most beautiful things about NYC is that even with its immense population, I still feel like the city is one big family. After Joe Allen's, I hail a cab and get back to my hotel room around midnight. What a beautiful and glorious day this was. What a major understatement that is!

I spend the next week looking for apartments. This being the first time in my life that I have had to budget my money, finding an apartment in my price range is proving to be a bit of a chore. My monthly allowance from Dad barely makes ends meet. I found a lovely apartment on Park Avenue and Thirty-Eighth Street that would have been ideal. Only, after adding up rent, electric, and all, my monthly allowance barely made it. If I could go without food, it might work. Sure, who needs food? I wanted to slim down a bit to star in *Oh Calcutta* anyway. I guess I will have to go to plan B. Plan B is to get a room at the Roger Williams Hotel (soon to be nicknamed the Roach Williams) directly across the street from the academy. I decide to get a roommate as well. I learn to adjust and it works out fine. My new roommate's name is Barry Herzog, an aspiring actor as well.

It's funny…the things you remember and the things you forget. The following is what I chose not to forget.

School day arrives. Sadly, during my first couple of weeks, the academy does not impress me as much as I had hoped. The vast majority of teachers appear to be out-of-work actors. It just does not feel as professional as I thought it would be, but I try to be as positive as I can and give it my best shot. The school year consists of two terms, each term putting you with a new group of people. A Deborah Wray from Chattanooga, Tennessee, was the only actor in both my terms. We performed scenes together often. I will always remember, during our second term, we did a scene from *The Lion in Winter*, which went extremely well. The entire class stood up and gave us a standing ovation when we finished. Deborah and I had excellent chemistry. She was a very special friend. We dated briefly that first year. I loved it when one day Deborah would tell me that her mother referred to me as her gentleman caller. It is like a scene from *The Glass Menagerie*.

One incident that I wish I could have erased happened the first month. Frances Fuller, one of the chosen alumni from the 1920s and still acting, was on the academy's board. At the end of the first month, Ms. Fuller was the star speaker at a welcome get-together. All of the first year's students were present. Ms. Fuller graced the small stage, and after a fifteen-minute speech, it was hinted that a student would be called to assist her in some way. To quote Ms. Fuller: "I'm an old lady, and I don't hear as well as I used to, so if I should choose you, please speak loud and enunciate where I can understand you." I, as well as the majority of the students, took her seriously. I was the chosen guinea pig and asked to join this grand dame. As requested, when asked to recite a chosen passage from a play, I spoke loud and  over-enunciated each syllable where our beloved speaker could hear me. Well, Ms. Fuller could not have been more insulted, saying, "How dare you behave in such a manner! Kindly get off this stage and I'll get someone who can read properly." I wish I had been man enough to say, "Ms. Fuller, this is what you asked us to do!" Only, I didn't. I curled back into my seat, stunned and embarrassed. Apparently, when Ms. Fuller made the "hard of hearing" statement she was just making a sick joke. When the end of this ghastly gathering arrived, one of the other teachers took me aside and whispered, "I would have done what you did." Only the grand dame will still depart thinking I was making fun of her. So much for her approval in my being asked back for the second year. That is one vote I'm sure not to get. What a bummer of a day!

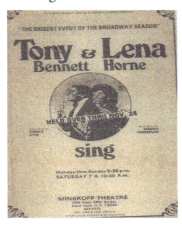

Even on a fixed allowance, this first year I did manage to squeeze in a Broadway show or two. I would have rather starved than miss a show. One evening I was able to get tickets to opening night of a Tony Bennett–Lena Horne concert. It was magnificent.

The show was the best! Lena and Tony were both magical!

I noticed that after the show, there was a line of people gathering to go to the escalator for some function. The function was the cast party for Lena and Tony. One naturally would have to have an invitation. I stood there in awe with my mouth open. After about fifteen minutes, one lady who looked like Joan Crawford but wasn't would fly up the escalator with no invitation. One of the security guards saw this, saying to me, "Hey, fellow, go ahead and go on up." I could not believe it! I was going to be part of their opening night party! There were stars everywhere! I refrained from approaching many of them, but I had to have my moment with a few of them. Lena, Tony, and Dionne Warwick were my chosen victims. I went up to Ms. Horne while she was talking to Dionne and just thanked her and told her how much I enjoyed the show. She thanked me, shaking my hand. Then I believe I then uttered to Ms. Warwick, "I love your work too." I was able to see Mr. Bennett, alone, and after complimenting him, he too shook my hand and thanked me. He was super!

One of my other major theater nights was when I took Deborah to see Maggie Smith and John Standing in Noel Coward's *Private Lives*. I surprised Deborah, hiring a limousine and chauffeur for the evening. The play was beyond brilliant! *Private Lives* is the story of a divorced couple who end up having adjoining suites during their second honeymoon with their new mates. There was a priceless moment when Maggie, as Amanda, sees her ex-husband Elliott in the adjoining suite. Instead of simply looking shocked, Maggie jumps backward ten to fifteen feet. It was priceless! I have seen *Private Lives* many times through the years, even with Elizabeth Taylor and Richard Burton, but this was the best! Dame Maggie Smith is not to be equaled.

A few weeks later, when Deborah and I were roaming around Greenwich Village, we were able to catch another grand dame in a one-woman show. We happened to walk by the New School and noticed a large crowd gathering at its entrance. Bette Davis was appearing in a one woman show chronicling her career. We, naturally, did not have tickets. With such a humongous crowd, the ticket takers were unable to keep some without tickets from entering the auditorium. Much to my delight we were able to sneak our way in. What an outstanding show! Ms. Davis would talk about her career in length with footage from her many movies displayed in the background throughout. What a life that talented icon had! "There's no business like show business."

A month or so later I was fortunate enough to see Ms. Joan Crawford appearing at the Town Hall on Forty-Third Street. She was appearing in a similar one-woman show discussing her brilliant and colossal career. Before the show's start, members of the audience were invited to write down any questions that one had for the grand dame, and the questions picked at random. I submitted one, and much to my delight, mine was one of the chosen questions. So halfway through the show, its commentator announces to Ms. Crawford, "John Strange asks the question, 'Do you have any advice for a young struggling actor, specifically me?'" (Note: He said my name wrong.) Ms. Crawford's response was "Get a good agent." I should have taken her advice seriously. I never did get a good agent. Maybe that's why I never made it.

The school year, surprisingly, went by rather quickly. Time flies when you're having fun. There were classes in drama, speech, and dance. I felt like I had done relatively well and absorbed all the teachings in a commendable way. But who knows?

April approaches. It is time for roles to be given out in the school's year-end play project. How one performs in these plays will be a determining factor in being asked back for the second year. I am not terribly pleased with the roles given to me. The role of Howard in *Picnic* is okay, but the other two from *Cat on a Hot Tin Roof* and *A Place in the Forest* are miniscule. How can I ever show my immense talent with such minor roles? As fate would have it, the fellow who had one of the major roles in *Forest* drops out, the role then given to me. Well, that makes things a bit better though it's still not much of a lift to my ego, not initially given the large role. Whatever!

Deborah is the mother, Flo Owens, in *Picnic*. A funny thing happened at dress rehearsal. At a most dramatic part when Flo Owens discovers her daughter, Millie, has been drinking whiskey, Deborah, as Mother Flo, comes out and yells incorrectly, "Who fed Millie to my whiskey?" I burst out laughing, which, needless to say, is not the most professional thing to do.

In *Picnic*, my director, Ciprion Gable, asked me to play Howard as more of a playboy type, which is totally different from the way it was played in the movie where Howard is rather shy and mousy. I felt the shy route would have been better, but having to follow directions, I did as I was told, trying to make Howard as much like Hugh Hefner as possible.

Well, I thought I did pretty well in all my plays, but of course, I naturally will not know for a month or two when I will receive my acceptance or refusal from the academy.

Sadly, June arrives and I am back in Dallas hopefully to return to NYC in September. I am miserable being back in Texas after my amazing year in New York. July arrives and I get a call from Deborah. She heard from the academy and she was accepted. I was thrilled for her. I swear her acceptance made me feel like I was accepted. I was overjoyed for her! So I should be hearing from the academy soon then. I get more and more excited with each day.

I hear from two of my other best friends from the academy, Debi Albis and David Alvins. Theirs was not good news. Neither was accepted. Damn! They both are so talented. What news awaits me?

On Friday, I go to the mailbox to find that much-anticipated letter. Excitedly, I hurry back into the house and open the letter. Frances Fuller got her revenge! I was not accepted! I was crushed and just could not believe it. I was near tears. I take that back, for I think I did cry. "Damn!" How could this be? My family, naturally, is very sympathetic. After a few hours I try to come out of my gloom and gather my composure. I spend the next week thinking of my next plan of attack. I have to get back to New York, or maybe I could try Hollywood.

I get a call from Dad. He asks me to come over to his house to discuss things. He is adamant that I quit this acting thing and consider a four-year academic college. I am so unhappy. I agree to his school terms, but only if I could be attending college in New York. He says no, for obvious reasons. "You'd be spending all your time trying to get back into acting! You have to go to college here in Dallas!" I am sick! What the hell can I do? I am nineteen years old without a penny in the bank. It kills me, but I give in. I agree to give a college in Dallas a try. I enroll in a community college and even take a course in drama, landing a lead role as Eilert Lovberg in their production of *Hedda Gabler*. Where there is a will, there is a way. However, even my success in their drama department does not make me a happy camper.

Then an idea hits me. If I am going to be in Dallas, I have to have a car to get around, so I nervously ask Dad if he will buy me one. He agrees, saying he will look into buying me a used car. Used? Did someone say *used*? Whatever!

I get my used car, which he puts in my name. This is quite nice! The car is in my name! This is very cool indeed! Whatever this car is worth is money in the bank to me. I am no longer without equity. A secret plot comes to mind. After a deadly nine months in Texas, I sell the car and, with the money, move back to New York!

It was a few years before Dad and I would speak again. He would never admit it, but I think Dad actually admires my determination. I inherited this trait from him.

I call Deborah and tell her the good news. I ask her if I could stay with her and her roommate, Sarah, for a month where I could get settled into my own apartment. She says sure. I make the proper flight arrangements and I am back to Manhattan.

It's so good to be back! I felt like I came alive the second the plane landed. The energy you feel in Manhattan is like nothing else in the world. It is so good seeing Deborah and all my old friends again. I end up staying in Sarah's apartment on Thirteenth Street for about a month.

At month's end, I take Deborah and Sarah to see *Over Here* with the Andrews Sisters to show my appreciation. I had seen it before, and they loved it! I also treat them to dinner at a wonderful new restaurant I have fallen in love with called Ted Hook's Backstage. It is the best, and stars frequent it every evening. Its decor is exceptional, looking so theatrical. Along with its tables and booths is a gigantic white grand piano with people seated around having cocktails. The multitalented Steven Ross is at the helm of the piano. He and I will become good friends as the years go by. Whenever a celebrity is spotted having dinner there, their name is always announced with a spotlight on them. I love it! Deborah and Sarah loved it too.

This summer I would also see *Gypsy* at the Winter Garden Theater starring Angela Lansbury. What an outstanding show that was! Is there anything that talented actress can't do. After the show, I waited with a large group of adoring fans, at the stage door, for her autograph. When she finally came out, she simply darted to her black limousine, muttering, "I'm sorry but I must rush. I've a dinner engagement." Hey! I always stop for my fans!

I find a small studio apartment on Eleventh Street and Sixth Avenue. I also landed a job on Wall Street with the law firm Winthrop, Stimson, Putnam, & Roberts. Talk about a mouthful! My job is rather minor in the copy room, making copies of all the lawyers' important documents. It is a bit boring, but it pays the bills. I find it most exciting working on Wall Street with all those stockbrokers.

Although I am working in a nine to five, I still try to take a daily peek in the trade papers. One of the New York papers advertising local auditions is *Backstage*. It is in *Backstage* that I find an audition for an Off-Broadway musical revue called *I Gave at the Office*. I audition for the role of a Texan. God knows I have had enough training to be able to deliver a dynamite Texas accent. The woman who wrote the review, Nina Prescott, and who is auditioning me loves my accent and gives me the part instantly. Nina will also be starring and directing it. Three other men are cast members as well. An exceptional pianist, Norman Fields, also a good friend of Nina's, will agree to be in the show. Norman is a most celebrated pianist! His talent with the keys is the best! I loved working with him! I hope that our revue will equal his immense professionalism. We will be performing at The English Pub located at Fifty-Seventh Street and Seventh Avenue. It is too bad the pub is not located one block over, which is Broadway. Then I could say I was playing on Broadway. Rehearsals are at Nina's apartment every other day after work. Tom Gattos, one of the other actors, is fantastic. He and I become quite close until his move out of NYC the following year.

A funny little thing happened one evening when Tom and I went to a double feature at a nearby theater to see a sneak preview of *Funny Lady* starring Barbra Streisand. *Funny Lady* followed *The Stepford Wives*. It was during the end, and the most dramatic part, of *Wives* when two men took seats in front of us. They were talking and gabbing nonstop and absolutely ruining my *Stepford* finale. Just before I pounce on the rude couple in my fit of rage, I kick the back of their two seats and get them to shut up. The two men turned out to be the New York critic Rex Reed and a friend. They were there to review *Funny Lady*. We found *Funny Lady* okay but not nearly as good as *Funny Girl*. I whispered my critique to Rex on my way out.

Getting back to *I Gave at the Office* after a month or a month and a half, we were ready for showtime. I was to sing two songs solo. I even drop my pants in one scene. Maybe it will get me a part in *Oh*

Calcutta. One night, in a mad rush, I accidentally forgot to put on my boxer shorts showing a bird's eye view of my little fella. Did I say little? I beg to differ. If that does not get me in *Oh Calcutta*, nothing will.

The opening night seemed to go fine, as well as the following three weeks. We never made Broadway, but it was a fun experience. *Backstage* did review the show. They gave Prima a nice review. My only mention was *"and one actor even drops his pants."* I told you my little fella would get me in the news.

Louis Maniscalco

It was at the end of the year that I developed a friendship with a Louis Maniscalco from Yonkers. We met in the Village one evening and became instant friends. I visited him in his apartment and would eventually move in with him. His rent was a mere fraction of mine. I tried adjusting to the daily work commute, but after a year, it was no dice. Daily travel to his apartment from work involved the subway and a bus. Ouch. I stuck it out for a year and then put my furniture in storage and moved back to the city.

I thought I would stay at the YMCA for a week or two before moving into a new apartment. I ended up staying at the Y for a year and a half. In the past, if anyone told me he was staying at the YMCA, it was as if he was telling me he had two weeks to live. I could not imagine such a predicament. At least *this* Y is on the east side. It is on Forty-Seventh Street between Second and Third Avenue. I cannot think of a better playground!

I have also switched jobs, at this point, and am now working for St. Claire's Hospital on the west side. My job is that of a clerk/data processor. I will be at this job for about a year and a half. As far as jobs go, I just have not found my niche yet.

JUNE 1975

It is a lovely Saturday afternoon in New York City. The sun is shining, the birds are singing, and millions of New Yorkers are rushing off to their chosen destinations. Life is good. I wake up at nine o'clock feeling exuberant and happy, like any moment Julie Andrews will fly by singing "My Favorite Things." It is a picture-perfect Saturday! Off to the bathroom for a quick shower and shave, and then on to Fifth Avenue. I first stop off at a nearby diner and have a bite to eat. Cooking was never and never will be one of my attributes, and now that I am living at the Y, it is hardly an option. Besides, nothing compares to a good old New York bagel with cream cheese.

I approach Fifth Avenue, among the scurrying hundreds, and begin my window-shopping. I have an audition Monday for another Off-Broadway show and would like to buy some chic outfit for the audition. Did I say Off Broadway? Try off, off, Off Broadway. This theater is in New Jersey. Anyway, after a couple of hours I find the Rhett Butler of outfits: a dark green shirt, tan shacks, and a smashing light brown jacket. Am I hot or what? The role I will be auditioning for is that of an English gentleman, so I am aiming to look as much like Noel Coward as possible. Perhaps I should purchase a charming ascot as well, but that might be overdoing it a touch. As I approach Fifty-Sixth Street, I stop at a bookshop. In the large front window is an elaborate display of its most recent best sellers, one of them being that of the long-awaited biography of Ms. Katharine Hepburn. Ms. Hepburn is admired so very much among my many actor friends. I was fortunate enough to see her perform Coco in 1970. What a talent! What a legend!

Deborah was one of the ones who admired her so. In fact, Deborah had heard that Ms. H. and Irene Selznick had been considering directing a movie based on the book *Martha*. Deborah thought she would be perfect for the lead role and would so much like to audition for it. Deborah's roommate at the time, Harriet Hayward, an aspiring actress as well, just happened to be taking singing lessons from Sue Seaton, Ms. Hepburn's singing teacher during *Coco*. Once during one of her lessons, Ms. Seaton decided to give Ms. H. a call and uttered the phone number out loud. Harriett quickly jotted the number down and then, naturally, gave it to Deborah and myself. What a break this is! Deborah could call her now and maybe arrange an audition, but alas, every time Deborah would call, Kate's secretary, Phyllis, would always answer her phone. Deborah just had to speak to Kate directly!

Well, it is back at the bookshop that I run to a phone booth to tell Deborah about the book:

DEBORAH: Hello.

JOHN: Debbie! It's John.

DEBORAH: Oh, hi! What's going on?

JOHN: You'll never guess what!

DEBORAH: You met Katharine Hepburn?

JOHN: No. Don't be silly. Her book came out, though.

DEBORAH: Great! Buy me a copy.

Excitedly, I buy a book for Deborah and me. Then I walk down Fifth Avenue and headed home, two books in one hand and my Rhett Butler outfit in the other. As I approach Forty-Ninth Street, it occurs to me that possibly this is the street that Ms. H. lives on. I know she is in Turtle Bay. I did see a picture of her house once, but so many New York townhouses look alike. I thought, maybe, I spotted one that looked like hers on the north side of the street, so I stake out a tree on the south side and begin my "Kate watch." Fifteen minutes later a car drives across and double-parks on the south side of Forty-Ninth Street almost where I am standing. I pay no attention to it, however, with my attention focused on her alleged house on the north. Two women, who I am hardly watching, begin taking various things from the car to their townhouse, going back and forth several times. A man, at this point, comes out of the townhouse, which I am standing in front of, and introduces himself. His name is Louis Vargas and he is Stephen Sondheim's gentleman's gentleman. I was standing directly in front of Stephen Sondheim's house! *"Send in the clowns."*

JOHN: *How are you?*

LOUIS: *Hi!*

JOHN: *Hi! I'm John Strangi.*

LOUIS: *I'm Louis Vargas. So what's doing?*

JOHN: *(shyly) Well, this will probably sound a bit silly, but I heard that Katharine Hepburn lived on this street, so I thought I'd just take a chance, and hang around a while and see if she...*

LOUIS: *(laughing) Well, there she is.* (He points to the two women in that car.)

The two women that had been getting in and out of that car were Kate and her secretary Phyllis. Kate is Stephen Sondheim's next-door neighbor. I am numb!

LOUIS: *Follow me and I will introduce you.* (Being under Mr. Sondheim's employ and living next door, they are well acquainted.)

With knees shaking, as they never have before, Louis takes me over to Kate.

LOUIS: *Kate, I would like you to meet my good friend John.*

(I cannot believe what is happening.)

KATHARINE: How do you do?

JOHN: Ms. Hepburn, I have always admired you so much!

KATHARINE: Thank you.

JOHN: I just bought your book.

KATHARINE: Oh please don't ask me to sign it. I don't do autographs.

JOHN: Oh, no, I wasn't. Um, I so much enjoyed you in Love Among the Ruins. *(This was a recent TV movie starring Ms. Hepburn and Laurence Olivier.)*

KATHARINE: Thank you. I had fun making it.

JOHN: Well, it is such a pleasure meeting you.

KATHARINE: Thank you.

Well, to say I am in a state of disbelief is the understatement of the year. I just met Katharine Hepburn! I met one of the greatest legends of all time! I thank Louis again, and he invites me to drop by his place anytime. He lives on the fourth floor of Mr. Sondheim's townhouse. It looks like I have struck gold! After gathering my thoughts as much as possible, I run to a nearby phone booth and call Deborah.

DEBORAH: Hello.

JOHN: Guess what, Debbie?

DEBORAH: What?

JOHN: I just met Katharine Hepburn.

DEBORAH: Stop it, John.

JOHN: No, it's true! I swear it! She just happened to be coming home while I was on Forty-Ninth Street.

DEBORAH: Come on, John!

JOHN: Really! And Louis Vargas, Stephen Sondheim's houseman, introduced me.

DEBORAH: John!

(At this moment, I notice that Phyllis has just returned to their double-parked car and proceeds to drive away.)

JOHN: Debbie! Debbie! Phyllis just drove away in their car! Now Kate will have to answer the phone. Call her! I'm serious!

DEBORAH: Well, okay.

Deborah immediately places the call but, upon hearing Ms. Hepburn's voice, freezes and says nothing. She is most upset with herself to say the least. There goes her one chance to speak with Kate directly and try to arrange an audition. Several days pass, and needless to say, Saturday's Hepburn incident keeps pressing on Deborah's brain. What could be her next plan of attack? The following week, Deborah calls Kate's house again and speaks with Phyllis. Phyllis tells her that she will relay her audition request to Ms. Hepburn. This gives Deborah hope but, just to be on the safe side, writes another letter to Ms. Hepburn as well.

A week goes by. Another week passes by. Now it has been an entire month! It is 10:00 a.m. on a Monday morning in July. Deborah is at work. Harriett, her roommate, is still half asleep. The phone rings. Harriett pushes her long blonde hair from her eyes and goes to the phone.

HARRIETT: Hello?

KATHARINE: Hello. Good morning.

HARRIETT: Yes?

KATHARINE: Is there a Deborah Wray there, please?

HARRIETT: Who is this?

KATHARINE: This is Katharine Hepburn and I'm calling for a Deborah Wray.

HARRIETT: Oh, well I'm afraid she's at work right now.

KATHARINE: Would you please tell her that I have called.

HARRIETT: Sure!

KATHARINE: And please ask her to get back to me.

HARRIETT: Of course!

KATHARINE: I'm sorry for disturbing you.

HARRIETT: No, not at all.

KATHARINE: Good-bye.

HARRIETT: Bye.

Well, this just cannot be for real! It just can't be happening. It is like a scene from a Hepburn/Tracy movie. Only it is real! Harriett calls Deborah at work, and as you would guess, Deborah is shell-shocked. She just cannot believe that this is actually happening. Deborah tries her best to pull herself together and collect her thoughts as best she can. She looks for a quiet spot to call Ms. Hepburn. Deborah finds the spot and makes the call. The audition is set for Saturday at 1:00 p.m. A star is born! We all hope.

Deborah arrives home from work around six and immediately starts calling all of her closest friends, me first, and telling them. We are all so excited for her! One of our own might be getting that big break, that break that we all dream of getting one day. This is so, so exciting!

Monday…Tuesday…Wednesday…Thursday…Friday…Talk about five of the longest days in history! However, alas, Saturday finally arrives and Deborah is off for her one o'clock appointment at 244 East Forty-Ninth Street.

Ms. Hepburn greets Deborah at the door and shows her in. She immediately asks Deborah if she would like a drink. "I have lots of liquor…booze everywhere!" Deborah naturally declines the offer. (I would have asked for a double.) Ms. H. hands her the script of *Martha* and invites her to look it over first, if she likes, and after a moment or two is asked to recite a passage from the script. All in all Deborah was probably at the townhouse about an hour. *Fairy tales can come true…*Deborah was not too happy with her reading, but then most of us actors never are.

Weeks pass as well as months, and sadly, there is no callback from Kate. Kate and Ms. Selznick's project of directing *Martha* was never to come to life. At least Deborah did not lose the part to some other girl. At least she did have her golden moment with Kate.

Louis and I will remain good friends for the next fifteen years and see a lot of each other. I will be having coffee in Sondheim's kitchen hundreds of times during the coming months. Louis was a great man. I met many fascinating people through him. He was charming! "Here's to the ladies who lunch."

Louis will take me to see *Chicago* starring Chita Rivera and Gwen Verdon. We were in the best of house seats, second row center. I am guessing he was able to obtain these exceptional house seats through Sondheim's connections, but I didn't ask. I thought the show was stupendous in every way. Chita and Gwen were superb. Chita's opening number rising from the ground was eye popping. I have loved Chita Rivera ever since I saw her in the movie *Sweet Charity*. What a great talent!

This Christmas, Louis will throw a nice party in his fourth-floor pad. He invites me to ask my Louis Maniscalco to the party. (Since we have two Louises here, I'll refer to Louis Manisacalo as Louie.) Louie is blown away! "I'm going to a Christmas party in Stephen Sondheim's townhouse!" He cannot wait! The party would begin around 6:00 p.m. with cocktails, which is close to the time we arrive. There must have been around twenty guests. A lovely buffet followed cocktails. We stayed until around ten, when I accompanied Louie to Yonkers. I spent the night at his place.

The next morning, during coffee, much to my dismay, Louie showed me a memento he had taken from Sondheim's house. From the small Christmas tree on the staircase, Louie had taken an ornament. I was a bit shocked and told him he should not have done that. Louie replied, "When will I ever be at Stephen Sondheim's house again?" Stephen, if you are reading this, I owe you $20. Well, since it is 1975, maybe I just owe you $5. What the hell, I'll send you $20.

1976

A MATTER OF GRAVITY

The lovely month of May has arrived. Summer is nipping at the door and overcoats have taken a rest. Around noon, I wander over to see Louis. He asks me if I would like to join him for lunch. I'd love to. He takes me to a wonderful restaurant-bar on First Avenue called the Mayfair. I love it! I find out that the Mayfair has been a watering hole of celebrities for years—Ethel Merman and Marilyn Monroe, to name a few. The Mayfair will become one of my favorite hangouts.

We head back to Forty-Ninth Street after lunch. Louis remembers that he has to ask Norah, Katherine Hepburn's cook, a question about something. He asks me if I would like to come along. Are you kidding? Of course, I want to come along.

Ms. H. is on tour now with the show *A Matter of Gravity*. I saw the show during its brief two-month run on Broadway. I heard Kate injured her ankle, closing the Broadway run early, and then going on tour. Kate would tour with the show playing her role in a wheelchair. Quite frankly, Kate's ankle was not the only injury to the show. I think the show stunk! It just was not any good, and most of my thespian friends agreed with me. When your name is Katharine Hepburn, you can get most anything to run. Just to spend an evening with such a grand dame is enough. Christopher Reeve was also in the original production.

Anyway, back at Kate's, Louis and I approach Kate's front door and greeted by Norah. She's a lovely lady somewhere in her late twenties, I guessed. We step into the kitchen. My eyes are that of a kid's in a candy shop, eyeing everything in sight. I cannot believe it! I am in Katharine Hepburn's kitchen! A kitchen is a kitchen is a kitchen. Her stove and refrigerator appear to be the originals dating back to the twenties when she bought the house. Did they have gas then?

Louis tells me later that whenever Kate has a gathering at her house, she always asks him if he would furnish the ice cubes. Kate's ancient refrigerator has no ice maker.

Ten minutes into our visit, Norah asks me if I would like a tour of the house. I, naturally, say yes. This is not to be believed! I am getting a tour of Katharine Hepburn's house! We first go into the living room. Like the kitchen, the furniture seems to be that of the Smithsonian vintage. This old, used look is really what I would expect from Kate. I see pictures of Spencer Tracy throughout. We then go upstairs, passing through several bedrooms. It is when we approach the top floor that my eyes do a major double take. On a very small table in the corner are Kate's three Oscars. I am in a state of disbelief. I first touch the one she received for *Morning Glory*. It, being from the Academy Awards' birth, is smaller and a different appearance than her other two from *The Lion in Winter* and *Guess Who's Coming to Dinner*. Louis then hands me the one from *Guess Who's Coming to Dinner*. I caress it like a newborn baby. It is heavier than I thought it would be. Sadly, after about a minute or two, I place the "baby" back into its cradle. What a thrill! Well, Norah will be on my Christmas list for life. We head downstairs to the first floor. I thank Norah again, and it is back to reality.

Another jolly episode occurred with Louis when I gave him his birthday present in Sondheim's kitchen. I surprised him with several alabaster clowns. Just as he opened them up, Stephen came downstairs to the kitchen. Seeing the clowns, he commented, "Send in the clowns." I find that priceless!

Thanksgiving this year offered a new experience for me. It was a cold November morning, and I decided that I would venture out to see the Macy's Thanksgiving Day parade in person. With my anticipation of the swarms of people I would have to battle to obtain a good position for the parade, I locked my position near Macy's around 7:00 a.m. I was under the impression that I would be beating the crowds, but I was dead wrong. Swarms of people had already gathered. Freezing and shivering in the cold, I stood for the next few hours. One by one the gigantic floats would pass me. Halfway through the parade, with Mickey Mouse hovering above, I decided this would be my one and only time seeing this spectacle in person. Hell, I would rather be on my living room sofa with my feet up watching on TV. Why go through this agony? At least I can say I saw it live once, but never again! Damn, it was cold! At its end, I walked back home, peering at Snoopy and his friends in the background and trying to keep the icicles from forming on my ears. How does Santa stand it!

1977

MISS MARGARIDA'S WAY

I have changed jobs and am now working at the Citi Athletic Club. I am told it's primarily a Jewish club. My job is that of the hat-coat check boy. Am I not moving up in the world? It is on the boring side, to say the least, but I adjust.

Many a celebrity graced its front door many times, Al Pacino and Max Gordon among them. Al Pacino was pleasant but struck me as extremely shy. After Al Pacino's one-time visit, I tore his autograph from the sign-in sheet. Max Gordon, one of Broadway's most stupendous theatrical producers, of the 1920s and 1930s, was charming. He lived on the same street as the club so was at the club often.

Mr. Gordon quickly became aware of my passion for acting and one day even tried to pull a few strings for me. Becoming a member of Actors Equity is no easy task, and he thought he could help me to become a member. He placed a call, raving about my immense acting talents, thinking that would be enough to open the door for me. Sadly, they refused, saying that no allowances could be made. I remember vividly his saying *"Don't you know who I am?"* The next week, Mr. Gordon does receive a letter from Equity apologizing and saying *"Yes, of course, we know you are and all the outstanding contributions you have given the theater."*

Through the years, I will never be able to make it into Actors Equity, but thanks to my work in television and movies, I do get into SAG-AFTRA.

Stanley Marcus, of Neiman Marcus fame, also graced the club's doors once. I was not quite sure what to say to him, but when he shook my hand, I uttered, "I love your store." I also told him I was born in Dallas. He was very nice and quite charming.

Elvis Presley died on August 16. I was never a big fan of his since his major status blossomed when I was blossoming myself. I was just a youngster. A woman I worked with at the club who had blossomed during his reign was very upset. She was a big fan of his. He was very talented.

Miss Margarida's Way, starring Estelle Parsons, was a favorite of mine, this year. It was a one-woman show. Ms. Parsons, as Miss Margarida, plays a schoolteacher, and the theater's audience members are her students. Class participation was encouraged. Surprisingly enough, I do not remember attempting to participate much, the ham that I am, but Ms. Parson's performance was brilliant!

1978

BALLROOM

When I fall in love with anything, I do not hesitate in showing it. That is what happened to me with *Ballroom*, the new Michael Bennett musical. It starred Dorothy Loudon and was Mr. Bennett's first Broadway show since his stupendous success with *A Chorus Line*. Its story is originally from the movie *Queen of the Stardust Ballroom*, starring Maureen Stapleton, only with lots of new music and dancing this time out. To sum it up, *Queen* is the story of a middle-aged woman who falls in love with a middle-aged man. They meet at the *Stardust Ballroom*.

Ballroom, opens at the Majestic Theater in December to mixed reviews. Actually, they were closer to bad reviews. I do not get it. I loved it! The choreography, dancing, singing, staging, and everything else about it, I found magical. I talked earlier about having chills every time I'd hear an overture. This show gave me the chills with each musical number.

Unfortunately, with its bad reviews, *Ballroom*, would only run for three months. I would go and see it thirteen times. I would get to meet Ms. Loudon on one of those evenings. What a charming and talented lady! I also met several of the cast members as well as Jonathan Tunic who conducted the orchestra. What a talent he is! He will go on to compose for many more musicals as well as movies.

Sadly, I think one of the negatives about *Ballroom* is that it is about older people. I do not know why, but I find now that any play or musical that focuses on the older generation really has to be more than a winner for it to last. That hurts now that, unfortunately, I am approaching that group. However, let us not even go there, please.

The year 1978 was also the year that casino gambling was approved and started in Atlantic City. Resorts was its first casino. I could not wait to go and check it out. I am hardly an experienced gambler, but I have to go see it. It is about a two-hour drive on the bus from Manhattan. All aboard! I take a 10:00 a.m., which arrives a bit after twelve. Full of excitement, I creep into the hotel and head to the casino. The haunting sounds of coins clinking and clanging in the hundreds of slot machines greet you at the door. I love it! I decide to try my hand at slot machines first and have a go at it. One particular machine catches my eye and it is up for adoption. That slot machine belongs to me for the next two hours. A hundred dollars later I roam and explore a bit. It is all so exciting!

I, next, decide to try my hand at blackjack. I knew how to play it but was less than familiar with its basics, the basics being when to hit and when not to hit. My inexperience soon becomes obvious to the fellow players at my table. One by one they leave to find a seat at another table. My immense charm was hardly enough to keep them there. They knew I was a novice. My heart goes out to all of them. I lost another hundred dollars, but it was fun. I have learned to think of gambling like going to a Broadway show. One pays for two to three hours of enjoyment. It is all about the moment. Oh, and please, we must not forget about the free cocktails one gets while playing. Is that cool or what? Whether it is at a slot machine of a blackjack table, the drinks are flowing.

Five o'clock arrives and it is back on the bus. Everyone expects to be going back a millionaire, but sadly, few accomplish such a feat. You always have to keep that one bit of hope that your dream might come true. It is very much like the theater.

MAJOR AUCTION OBSESSION BEGINS

March 1 will mark the beginning my major obsession with auctions.

Christie's was auctioning the personal property of Joan Crawford. I loved the rich excitement of bidding. I found it thrilling. Not having much of a bankroll, I really could not bid too heavy. I almost won a batch of Ms. Crawford's monogrammed napkins. The bidding was between me and one other fellow. It got all the way up to $800. Unfortunately, I gave up and let the fellow win. The agony of defeat is born! I left Ms. Crawford's auction with only an autographed picture. I do not enjoy losing, thank you very much, but do find the bidding so very exciting!

This is the year that I will begin taking acting classes at the HB Studios in Greenwich Village. The HB Studios is better known as the Herbert Berghoff studios. Mr. Berghoff is a very well-known actor/director. His celebrated wife is Ms. Uta Hagen. I will study there on and off for the next seven years. William Hickey, who years later is nominated for an Oscar in the movie *Pritzzi's Honor*, is one of my acting teachers. A lovely lady, Sunny Kreis, will be one of my acting partners and will remain a friend for life.

Sunny and I will, one weekend, get tickets for *The Kingfisher*, starring Rex Harrison, Claudette Colbert, and George Rose. I was excited getting to see the original Henry Higgins. I had never seen Ms. Colbert in anything before, but early on, did see Mr. Rose in *My Fat Friend*, starring Lynn Redgrave. *The Kingfisher* was good but nothing to write home about. Sunny wanted to stand by the stage door after and see if she could get a snapshot of a star or two. Ms. Colbert came out, hardly acknowledging us, and grandly approached her waiting limousine. As she got into her backseat, Sunny started to take that snapshot when Ms. Colbert yelled, "Don't you take that picture!" Maybe she was afraid Sunny would take her photo showing her left profile. I read where she would never allow pictures taken of her left side. I thought I was vain!

THIRTY-THIRD ANNUAL TONY AWARDS

The Antoinette Perry Awards

I had never been to the Tony Awards before. With my immense love of *Ballroom*, I wanted to attend this year to show my support. The awards were on June 3 at the Shubert. I purchased a ticket as soon as possible. A seat then cost a mere thirty-five dollars. I still have the receipt. With it, naturally, a black-tie event, I went out early to find a tuxedo to rent. I found mine at a cute little tailor shop on Sixty-Fourth Street. I tried on three or four before finding the perfect fit. Success! Move over, Cary Grant! Move over, Rock Hudson!

Evening approaches and I hail a cab to the Shubert Theatre where the awards are being held. Crowds and crowds of people are swarming the theater. I inch my way through all the men and women, feeling oh so important, and enter the theater. Before taking my seat, I choose to simply stand and do a bit of stargazing. Angela Lansbury! Joel Grey! Alexis Smith! "The joint is jumpin'!" As eight o'clock approaches, I take my seat. I am upstairs in the balcony, which is fine. The overture plays and it is on with the show. The hosts, this year, were Jane Alexander, Henry Fonda, and Liv Ullmann. Dorothy Loudon opens the show performing "Fifty Percent" from *Ballroom*. The presenters, as always, were some of Broadway's best. Ellen Burstyn, Al Pacino, Jack Lemmon, and John Houseman were among the many. (Maybe Mr. Houseman will grant me another *Julliard* audition.)

Sweeney Todd, Stephen Sondheim's new musical hit, dominated. It won the majority of the major awards. *Ballroom* only won one award, it being for choreography, and very well deserved, I must say. They had to win for that!

They're Playing Our Song, starring Robert Klein and Lucie Arnaz, walked away empty-handed as well. The show, the book, its director, and Mr. Klein received nominations, but none won. Lucie Arnaz should have at least been nominated, for I thought her performance was outstanding.

What great fun being a part of such a special evening. As you might have guessed by now, my next two targets were Sardi's and Backstage. I loved going to my two favorite restaurants in black tie. Both were filled to the hilt with people who had just attended the Tony Awards. I started out at Sardi's and ended the evening with cocktails seated around the piano at Backstage. What a glorious evening!

1980

SEEMS LIKE OLD TIMES

This year was the year of my long-awaited departure from the YMCA. I'm rather amazed that I lasted as long as I did. As fate would have it, Deborah was also looking to move, so we thought we might shack up together. We checked out houses around Sheepshead Bay, Brooklyn. After much searching, we found a house in Brighton Beach that was renting their top, second floor. Of course this means I am back to commuting again each day to work, but it might work. We sign the lease and are Brooklynites for a year.

John Strangi Deborah Wray

One weekend, before we moved in, I paid a visit to Louis in Yonkers. I always enjoyed my visits with him. During my visits, I would always find it so disturbing the way his next-door neighbors would treat their cat. Every visit I would hear that poor cat howling in agony, so on this visit I stole the cat. All right, so I'm a thief! Shoot me! Deborah and I would now be parents of a kitty. We named him Kitty. Very original!

I was never much of a cat person, but I really grew to love Kitty. Deborah and I had a fun year living together. We always had a good rapport. Our landlords weren't too happy with Kitty, though. They said he jumped around too much and made too much noise. Oh, please! How can a one-pound cat make that much of a racket? They adjusted.

One little incident with Kitty, which I *painfully* remember, was when he jumped out of the window onto a tree. With Deborah looking on, I inched my way onto the tree to rescue Kitty when all of a sudden Kitty leaps toward me, his claws grabbing ahold onto my shirtless chest. He was literally hanging from my chest. Deborah told me later, during my agony, I blurted out the words "I'm ruined." Kitty and I both survived.

It was fun living so close to the water. We would take walks by the seashore on occasion and even visit Coney Island every so often. Sheepshead Bay was also a lovely community and well within walking distance.

Mary Chapman John Strangi and Kitty

Deborah and I both decided that one year in Brooklyn was plenty and made plans to go our separate ways at the end of our lease. Who is going to keep Kitty, though? Deborah's best friend from Chattanooga, Mary Chapman, paid us a visit during our last month. We had a great time going to the horse races and doing all tourist things. With my move back to the city, I wasn't sure that my new city lifestyle would work with Kitty, so on Mary's return drive to Chattanooga, I offered him to Mary. Deborah and I created a makeshift cage for Kitty's ride in the backseat of Mary's car, and it was "Ta-ta Tabby." Kitty had become more than just a pet. A tear or two was shed. (By me, not Kitty.)

I was excited to be moving back to the city! I found a wonderful studio apartment on Sixty-First Street between First and Second Avenues. I love the building! It looks like a red schoolhouse. I am on the first floor in the front. There are ornate bars on all the windows. My rent is a bit more than I can afford, but I think I can make it work.

Late summer I had an interview with a stock brokerage on Wall Street. Not having any experience or knowledge of brokerage, my doubts of obtaining this one were many, but I landed it! This Canadian firm, Burns, Fry & Timmins, is located at 100 Wall Street. They hired me instantly after two interviews. I will be working in their P&S department.

1981

WOMAN OF THE YEAR

My new job with BF&T is actually not a nine to five. During my first couple of years, it is more like a nine to nine or ten. Hey! I am young and full of energy, and I want to learn everything I can about the stock market. I remember distinctly that even with those insane hours, my coworkers and I would still end the workday with a drink or two at the local pub.

**John Strangi and
Michele St. John**

When I was able to grab an evening free, I would still try to see one or two new Broadway shows. This was the year of Lauren Bacall's return since her triumph in *Applause*. Her musical this year was Kander and Ebb's *Woman of the Year*. Michele St John, from Texas, was paying me a visit along with her daughter, Chelsea Minguez. Michele's married name is Minguez. We were able to catch one Saturday night's show. The singing! The dancing! The choreography! All were superb! What a super show. Then to top it off we were able to meet Ms. Bacall at Sardi's after the show. She just happened to be at a table close to the downstairs bar. I approached her table, muttered that I hoped I wasn't intruding on her evening, but just had to tell her how much I enjoyed her performance in *Woman* and thanked her. She shook my hand and thanked me.

Oh, and Michele met Raquel Welch in the ladies lounge during intermission of *Woman*. Is that cool or what? Ms. Welch just happened to be seeing the show. They exchanged a few words.

I will only be in my Sixty-First Street apartment for a year. Once again, I stupidly don't renew my lease at its year's end and move in with a new *friend* in Redbank, New Jersey. When will I ever learn? That's the second dynamite apartment I have given up in the city! My New Jersey bout only lasted about seven months and I am without an apartment again.

Before my split up from my Redbank *pal,* I took out a loan of $5,000 to help the bastard. He had said he would pay me back— only, naturally, did not. For the entire next year, I will work two jobs daily to pay back my loan: one job nine to five and one job six to ten.

I briefly move in with a new roommate, Tony, in Newark, New Jersey, which is a zillion times closer than Redbank. Tony is a very nice fellow and has a very impressive apartment.

After a few months, I am in the subway heading for downtown. I am now donning a beard and mustache and seated next to a fellow with the same. We start a conversation during which he tells me his name is Ron, he lives in Greenwich Village, and that he is looking to sublet his apartment for a year and will most likely not be asking for it back. He is joining a monastery with hopes of becoming a monk. Ron invites me to look at his pad. The next day, I do just that. With this apartment coming furnished, I will have to leave my furniture in storage, but I love it and tell him it is a done deal. This is great! I love the Village! I take the subway train back to New Jersey and tell Tony of my find and that I will have to move out. He more than understands, wishing me all the best. I will be moving in on the first of next month.

1982

TORCH SONG TRILOGY

John Strangi Linda Zecchino

I'm so excited! My new Village apartment is so much closer to work as well! I become the best of friends with Linda Zecchino, a girl who lives on the second floor. She's crazy and a lot of fun. Linda will get in the habit of throwing rocks at my front window. Perhaps I should say pebbles. She was not out to break anything. She is just a crazy lady! Linda is Charles Osgood's secretary at CBS. She has already lived in this building a number of years. This apartment complex consists of one four-story front building plus a four-story back building. Both buildings are walk-ups.

I very much love living in Greenwich Village. There are so many charming cross streets with equally charming restaurants and cafés. There are a great many nightclubs as well where one is invited to take the microphone and sing a song or two. Five Oak's would become one of my favorites. It was a speakeasy during the 1920s and '30s. There is a wonderful black singer/piano player there every evening, Marie Blake. What a talented lady she is!

This was the year of my tenth-year high school reunion. I flew to Dallas for it. It was good seeing everyone. Doyle even joined us. I was especially happy seeing her.

With Ron having convinced me so that he would not be returning, I do not hesitate in investing money into the apartment. Mistake! My year's sublet ends and Ron does return and wants his apartment back. Bastard! He was so sure he would not be returning. There is a

John Strangi and Doyle

happy ending, though. In the back building, an apartment becomes available at the same time and I snatch it. This one is even bigger than Ron's. It is on the top floor. Alleluia! Things are looking good. I call storage immediately and arrange to have all my furniture moved to the back building. This is super! Everything happens for the best and this proves it.

Mystery Man John Strangi Joe Ammendolio

This year was also the beginning of the Greenwich Village Halloween parade and I participated in it. A good *friend* of mine, Joe Ammendolia, was to give an outstanding Halloween party that evening. I could not decide what to go as when I came across a large refrigerator box in the front of my apartment building. Eureka! I will go as a gift box. It was a hit! I even created a flap in the front when Mother Nature calls.

1983

LA CAGE AUX FOLLES

This was the year of the flood. This flood would only be affecting my apartment building. Just call me Noah.

It was on a lovely Saturday afternoon that Linda would pay me a visit. I commented to her that my toilet was making a strange noise every so often. So many buildings in New York City were constructed during the Stone Age, so one expects its antique plumbing to act up on occasion. Today was my day. Linda said that her toilet made the same noise, and all you had to do was make a small adjustment on a back pipe. I did not act on this immediately, but a couple of hours later I thought I would try it. With much reluctance, I entered the bathroom and approached that chosen pipe. As I played with its nozzle, the pipe broke, sending water gushing out nonstop. Old Faithful had erupted! Water is now streaming from my bathroom to the living room and finally the bedroom. I can't stop the damn thing! I panic! I am a nervous wreck! This cannot be happening! I call the fire department! I call Linda! Linda tries to calm me down, but unsuccessfully. Water is now streaming down the walls of all the apartments underneath mine. What a nightmare! This is too much! I am a mess. Water is gushing out nonstop—super, super strong.

The firefighters finally arrive. One of them calmly goes into my bathroom, asking me to follow him. He points to the pipe. "All you needed to do to stop the water was turn this little nozzle." I do not believe this! This whole nightmare could have been avoided with one little turn of the screw. I thank the firemen, having to keep from kissing one of them, and send them on their way.

Soaked, and with nerves still totally shaken, I attempt to put some order back into my apartment. What a mess! Where does one begin? Everything is soaked! I begin drying things off as best I can. I attack each of my tiny rooms, one by one, tackling the bathroom, the kitchen, the living room, and finally the bedroom. I am still in utter disbelief of all that just happened. Linda pours me a drink to help calm me down. It hardly does the trick.

I shower and try my best to get myself back together. I need an escape. I think I'll see a Broadway show? Perfect! I cannot think of a better way to escape all this madness. I call and see if I could get a ticket for *La Cage Aux Folles* at the Palace. Eureka! I got one. Six o'clock arrives and it's time for fantasyland. I am off. As always, I go to Sardi's first for a quick drink. A tiny triple would do me nicely, but I settle on my usual vodka martini. Never after today have I felt I needed one so desperately. Mmm-mmm, good!

It is off to the Palace at seven thirty. My seat, center orchestra, could not be better. The overture begins and it's curtain up. What a magnificent show. Jerry Herman is a genius! The show is perfection in every way. Those guys/girls were amazing! They were all gorgeous! The dancing and choreography were all beyond spectacular. Is there anything Jerry Herman cannot do? He has the golden touch without question.

I finish the night off at Sardi's. After a drink, for dinner I had their chicken a la Sardi's, which has always been my favorite. I then hightailed it to Backstage for one last cocktail. Hermione Gingold was dining there. I have always loved her. Then it is back to Old Faithful. I can only hope that things have dried. Remains of this day are still present. It is time to just grab a towel and go to bed.

It was this year that I also caught Elizabeth Taylor and Richard Burton in *Private Lives*. What a treat to see two superstars on stage together. As much as I adore that play, the two legends did not seem to do Sir Noel's play justice. It just did not work, but frankly, who the hell cares? They just do not make legends like the two of them anymore.

I also met Charles Osgood this summer. I was uptown on Fifty-Seventh Street, not far from CBS Studio's, and saw him crossing the street. I immediately approached him and told him that I was friends with his secretary, Linda Zecchino. I spoke with him for a good five minutes before realizing that instead of showering him with compliments, I had spent every minute talking about Linda. He was cool with that, sharing my fondness and praise of Linda.

(Years later, John and I will have Linda and Jean Wood, Charles Osgood's wife over for drinks and dinner. Jean is a pistol and so much fun! Love the lady!)

A MOON FOR THE MISBEGOTTEN

THE WIZ

THE RINK

John Strangi

Things are going quite well at work. I think this job is a fit. I am enjoying working in the madcap world of the stock market. All of my coworkers are grand and fun to work with. Two of the girls, Camille and Karen, are originally from one of "the islands," and most of the other men are locals. Richard Lammatina is a hoot, and I am especially fond of a Joey Robles. They are all a lot of fun. We have about six or seven stockbrokers. They are in their own little room. Their ages range from the early thirties to late fifties.

With my pocketbook being a bit more impressive, I am now able to fit in more Broadway shows. *The Wiz*, an all-black version of *The Wizard of Oz* was a delight! *The Rink*, starring Liza Minelli and Chita Rivera, was another super musical. My friend, Michele, was visiting from Texas and we saw this one together. Chita would win a more-than-deserved best actress Tony award for it.

A Moon for the Misbegotten, starring Colleen Dewhurst, was brilliant. I had always been an avid fan of Ms. Dewhurst! She is and always has been one of Broadway's best! This production was to offer me an experience I had never had in the theater before, though.

During one of its most dramatic scenes, a man in the audience had a heart attack, naturally stopping the show. Ms. Dewhurst, out of character, naturally, walked to the edge of the stage and loudly asked if there was a doctor in the house. Not that it was a surprise but it was interesting to see the cast members go in and out of character like that. Paramedics would eventually arrive with the ailing man taken out on a stretcher. The show would later continue, taking off where they left off. With the millions of people going to the theater, such an occurrence must happen every so often. I had just never been a party to one before. "The show must go on!"

I will also be attending the premiere of the movie *The Cotton Club*, on December 2 in Albany, New York. Friends of mine, who live in Albany, invited me. It was exciting attending the opening, but I didn't really think the movie was very good. Most of the critics agreed with me.

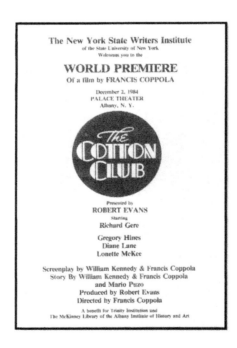

1985

JERRY'S GIRLS

For those of you who couldn't read between the lines, I switched from Juliet to Romeo years ago.

John Castagna and John Strangi

This will be my last full year of living in Greenwich Village. I met a John Castagna one evening in the Village. John is about ten years older than I am. A mutual friend introduced us, but we had seen each other around these last years. John has been head of window display–interior design at Lord & Taylor for many years. He seems like a dynamite fellow. John has an apartment downtown near Wall Street.

I had barely known John a month when he agrees to switch apartments with me for a week. Is this John a nice fellow or what? My sister, Jeanne, who has been physically challenged her entire life, is paying me a visit and since my Village apartment is a walk-up, her having to maneuver up and down stairs would be too much. John's building downtown is with elevators.

Jeanne spends a lovely week with me. I love it when people come to visit. It is as if I am seeing New York for the first time through their eyes. We did all the touristy things: Sardi's, the Empire State Building, the World Trade Center, Top of the Sixes, etc. We even went to Atlantic City one weekend. She loved playing the slot machines! I think she even made more money than I did. That's par for the course.

John eventually asks me to move in with him. This time, due to my many past impulsive moving blunders, I wait a year until my lease is up and I have tested the waters first. With my working on Wall Street, my living in that area would be ideal, but what's the rush? Does this logical way of thinking mean I've matured? I doubt it.

When not hanging out in the Village and downtown, John and I will naturally try to catch a Broadway show now and then. One of my favorites this year was a musical revue highlighting the music of Jerry Herman called *Jerry's Girls*. It starred Dorothy Loudon, Carol Channing, and Leslie Ughams. I loved it! I found it magical. Its reviews were mediocre, and it did not receive any major kudos at the Tony Awards, but I found it brilliant!

John and I will also begin frequenting downtown's Little Italy. John is Italian, and many from his family grew up in that area. Even though I am Irish-Italian, I do not think I experienced true Italian culture until I moved to New York. My Louis in Yonkers was my first intro to it, but John's family is at the top of the list. After one evening's dinner with John's parents, I think of them as my own. They are charming. His mother, Helen, is gorgeous and looks very much like Hedy Lamar. What a lovely, lovely, woman she is! Throughout all the following years, I will feel like she is my second mother. She possesses all of the sweet, loving, and caring qualities that John has as well. Like mother, like son.

John will also introduce me to the Hamptons. I had never been there before, and he has been going there for years during the summer. One of his dearest and oldest friends, Jeremiah Goodman, has a magnificent house in East Hampton. We will stay there during this summer when we can. Mr. G. is a most celebrated artist. His expertise with an easel and paintbrush is not to be matched.

I did fall in love with the Hamptons. The ride there in the train is a bit of a chore but well worth it in the end. It is a charming town with magnificent scenery!

Jeremiah Goodman's East Hampton House

1986

GOOD-BYE, GREENWICH VILLAGE, AND HELLO, PEARL STREET

May 31, 1986, was the final day of my lease on Cornelia Street in Greenwich Village. I will then move in with John on 333 Pearl Street in Lower Manhattan. It is a nice one-bedroom, and we will be happy there for the next seven years before our move uptown. I adjust quite well to living downtown. Once again, it is super being so close to my job. I even do go home for lunch on occasion. Is that cool or what?

More responsibility was given to me at work, so many of those lengthy workdays still exist, and yes, the workdays are still ended at the local bar. One evening the traders let me join them for cocktails at the New York Athletic Club on Fifty-Ninth Street. I loved it! What a super club! It has been there forever.

I still, and never will be, much of a master in the kitchen. Cooking just is not my thing. Why even bother with a restaurant on every corner in New York. If John and I are not dining in Little Italy or Chinatown, our destination is usually the Village. Occasionally we would venture to the Upper East Side.

A funny thing happened at the end of my first year, living on Cornelia Street in the Village. One day I decided to cook something in the kitchen. Only, the oven was not working. I called the property owner to complain. To which he replied, "I've been waiting a whole year for you to say something."

This summer will be the first of many spent in the Hamptons. Traveling two and one half hours to go anywhere just never appealed to me, but the magic of the Hamptons changed that. We would always stay at Jeremiah's house. Jerry, as most of us call him, would always throw the best of parties.

One weekend Jerry took us over to Edward Albee's house in Montauk. What a gorgeous house right on the ocean. He and Jerry have been friends for years and years. What a thrill meeting Edward. The man wrote *Who's Afraid of Virginia Woolf* for God's sake! We will be seeing much of Edward in the years to come. Edward's partner/ mate, Jonathan Thomas, is a sweetheart as well. What a handsome couple they are!

1987

JUST A SPOONFUL OF SUGAR

Dame Julie Andrews

As I mentioned earlier, I have been in love with Julie Andrews ever since *Mary Poppins*. I think I have seen *Mary Poppins* ten times, *The Sound of Music* twelve times, *Thoroughly Modern Millie* nine times, and *Star* eight times. I know *Star* was not too much of a success, but Ms. Andrews could not have done a better job with it. Every musical number performed was golden! I think its script was the culprit.

Anyway, with *Millie*, during my youngster days, I would be showing my immense theatrical love and, surprisingly, memorizing every word of the movie. I had remembered every single line, and I wrote it out to prove it to the world. Does this demonstrate a superior talent I possess, or should a room be reserved for me at Bellevue? Whatever! After much research, I was able to find an address for Ms. Andrews and mailed her my *Millie* script. A month or so later I did receive an autographed picture from her. She might have at least invited me to lunch!

My chance to see the divine Miss Julie in person was finally to occur. She was to perform a one-woman show at the Westbury Music Fair, outside of New York, on November 21. I immediately purchased tickets for John and me. I am so excited! We borrow John's father's car and drive out to Westbury. We arrive at the theater around seven o'clock for the eight o'clock show. The theater-auditorium is jam-packed with Julie fans.

Eight o'clock approaches, lights dim, overture plays, and Ms. Andrews appears. Wow! This is too much! There she is in person! She looks beautiful! All of the audience is so excited; you could hear a pin drop. She begins singing songs from her many, many movies, each one sounding priceless. What a treat hearing this in person! I did not want the evening to end. What a special evening and another New York golden moment. The hills are alive!

As far as Broadway shows go for this year, John and I would catch the wonderful musicals *Me and My Girl* and *Les Misérables*. Both of these shows would walk away with many a Tony award. They were golden!

In June, we had tickets for *Blithe Spirit*, starring Richard Chamberlain and Geraldine Page. A few weeks before our slated evening with *Blithe*, John and I just happened to walk past the theater to find Ms. Page exiting the stage door to a waiting limousine. I saw this moment as my perfect chance to meet this grand lady of the American theater, so I played like we had just seen the show and complimented her on her sterling performance. She thanked me, shaking my hand. I then proceeded to escort her to her limousine, opening its door for her. What a thrill to meet such a legend! Sadly, Ms. Page died a few days before our night's tickets. I had no desire seeing it without her starring in it, so I cancelled our tickets. That is another of the great legends gone. How much I admired her work! She was irreplaceable!

1988

PRINCE CHARLES ESCAPES AN AVALANCHE IN SWITZERLAND

Hey! We All Have Our Problems!

This year I turn thirty-five years old. I thought I would be much more of a success by now, but I suppose it is how one defines "success."

Even with my job, I still try to fit in an audition when I can. I auditioned for a commercial one week. I was number 280. Sadly in NYC, given such a big number is the norm. I, naturally, did not receive a callback. Rejection! Rejection! Rejection!

BFT, the company I work for, has changed locations. We are still downtown but now on Pine Street, which is in the vicinity of Wall Street. I was to learn that even when one works in the Wall Street area, but on a different street, one still says you work on Wall Street.

I also belong to a wonderful downtown gym, which I have also grown to love. My day now usually begins with my waking up before 6:00 a.m. where I can work out before work. I have taken a great love for running. I try to run a minimum of five miles a day. After my hour's run, I then try to work out with weights for an hour or so. I much prefer working out before work instead of after. The only barbell I want to hold after work is a martini glass.

The Phantom of the Opera was this year's hit musical. It opened to rave reviews, and I'm guessing it will be around till I'm old and gray. John and I got tickets for it one evening, and it was truly spectacular. What a spectacle! Its choreography is like no other. I think Andrew Lloyd Webber might anticipate his caricature being on Sardi's walls in the very near future.

1989

I'M READY FOR MY CLOSE UP, MR. DE MILLE

Congratulations

JOHN STRANGI
on landing the role
of the prison guard

in

GUIDING LIGHT
868-1162

February 23, 1989, is a day that will go down in history. No, it's not the day we landed on the moon or the day that Elvis Presley was born. It is the day when I landed my first soap opera.

It was during one of my evenings at Sardi's that I met a charming fellow who knew some of the bigwigs at ABC. He would give me a name to call to arrange an interview the week before.

I call and arrange my interview with a Jimmy of "Guiding Light." During my lunch break at work, I take a cab to ABC and meet with casting. Is this exciting or what? I have been assigned the role of a cop/prison guard and asked to report to the set on the morning of February 23. I'm also informed that if I work more than one day, I'll have to join AFTRA, the TV union. That is fine by me. I will work as many days as wanted. I kept a diary.

FEBRUARY 23

7:00 a.m.–I never thought that this day was going to come. At last, it's here! I have decided to call in to work sick today. I need the morning to relax and to prepare. Please let everything go better than good.

7:45 a.m.–I called work, acting sick, freeing the day for my first acting job.

8:55 a.m.–It is time to begin my transformation: snip, snip here; snip, snip there.

9:15 a.m.–Mustache looks great!

10:42 a.m.–Time to shave! All of the excitement is taking off!

I actually don't have to report to the studio till two thirty. Where's that martini?

2:30 p.m.–I report to the studio, immediately going to the fourth floor where the casting director is supposedly stationed. I tell the receptionist that I am here to see a Mr. Bohr. The receptionist had apparently just had her daily quotient of cocaine, for when I asked to see the man, she didn't seem to even know who he was. After regaining her consciousness, she pointed me to the direction of his office. *"Follow the yellow brick road."*

I arrive at Mr. Bohr's office. He is a nice guy and probably about my age. We talk for quite a while. We talked for so long; I was even beginning to feel like I was losing my voice. I was sounding a bit hoarse like a male Tallulah Bankhead. *Thank you, darling!*

I leave him and report to the fifth-floor wardrobe department and was told to report to the sixth-floor wardrobe department, and then told to report to the fifth-floor wardrobe department, and again told to report to the sixth-floor wardrobe department. What the hell are they doing to me? I am just a novice for Christ's sake! Finally, I am given my costume, which is a police uniform. I am then to report to dressing room number 3. Don't you love it? I proceed to the corridor to find a hall full of dressing rooms. I see a room number 5. I see a room number 4. Johnny does not see a room number 3. I summon an attendant to try to solve my maddening problem. The number 3 dressing room did not have a number on its door. Was the number

3 dressing room before number 4 and number 5? No, it was after number 5. That makes perfect sense!

I stroll casually into my long lost room, immediately taken by the bubble neon lights surrounding the mirror. It is all so theatrical! I slip on my police officer's uniform and look at myself in the mirror. "Is this guy hot or what?" I look great!

LIGHTS! CAMERA! ACTION!

The scene takes place in a prison. I am one of several policemen. There are also two prisoners. My directions are to walk back and forth from a bulletin board. "When he says this, walk four spaces left."  "When he says that, walk two spaces right." "When he walks to the table, walk four spaces toward him." The thing that I find a bit frustrating and nerve-wracking is that, not having seen a full script, I have no idea exactly when he will say this or when he will say that and when he will walk to the table, but I manage somehow. With the exception of not walking fast enough on one cue, things went rather smoothly.

John Strangi

All of the backstage work involved overwhelmed me. The cameras! The lights! The scenery! Honestly, I think the actors are secondary to all of the "behind the scenes" folk. Without those bones, that chicken ain't going anywhere. This shoot was over in a few hours. There would be another shoot later on. I have no way of knowing if I will be seen or not in this one. With so many cameras it is impossible to know. With a few hours before our next shoot, they said I could change clothes if I liked. After changing out of my costume, I proceeded to the green room. The entire cast of *"Guiding Light"* was watching themselves on the TV. I peeked in the door and being a novice really was not sure if I should join the pros or not. I entered anyway. It was interesting watching themselves with some analyzing their performance out loud. When the telecast ended, the room emptied out rather quickly. I am alone with Phil Donahue, not in person, but on the TV. After my hour with Phil, I decided to stroll outside and just walk a block or two before the next shoot. Here I am walking down the street with full makeup on! What will people think? Oh hell, this is New York, for God's sake! They will not think anything.

The next shoot takes place around 6:00 p.m. This one will only last for about an hour or two. The directions given, this time, are similar to the last. Hell, I am pro now! This take seemed to go much quicker with few retakes.

At the end of the evening, I am given a number, told to report to the fourth floor, and fill out my W4 form where I can be paid. I was number 7. That is lucky number 7! I do not know how, but I managed to get lost going to the fourth floor, eventually finding it. My talent amazes me. If called to shoot for a second day, it will be necessary to join the union AFTRA. Oh, please! Oh, please! Oh, please!

My wish came true. I get that call and join the Union. "One Life to Live" and "As the World Turns" will be my next two soaps. Don't you love it? I am working with the plural now. I will be working on and off for them during this entire year. I will be playing a maintenance man and a gym stud. I was a hit at them all, though when my Aunt Selma saw me as the maintenance man, she commented that I did not know how to hold a mop. I adore my new home away from home. With my second acting job, I confessed at work and told them the truth, making it easier to get the days off. Actually, the casting director for *One Life* wanted me to work more than I was, but sadly, I did not comply. Looking back, I wish I had agreed to her request. She even had me read for a speaking role once, but I did not get it. She said she actually needed someone younger. "Rude!"

Dixie Carter at the Café Carlyle

Also during this year, I began taking singing lessons from the celebrated pianist John Wallowitch. I had gone to see Dixie Carter's act at the Carlyle, which was outstanding. I saw it several times. I loved it so much that, during one her performances, I snuck in my tiny tape recorder and recorded the entire show.

During her act, she mentions that when she moved to New York City as a young girl, she immediately took singing lessons from a John Wallowitch who then lived in Greenwich Village. They would remain the best of friends through the years. I took this as my cue and sought to find him and see if he was still giving singing lessons. Eureka! He was. He now lives in a lovely apartment in Beekman Place. Bertram Ross, Mr. W's partner, met me at the door my first day. Mr. Ross is a most-celebrated dancer in the theater, having worked under Martha Graham for years and years. I will be studying with Mr. W for the next nine months and creating an act with him as well.

I will be performing my act at the Trocadero in Greenwich Village on December 1 and 2. I worked very hard trying to create the perfect act. Mr. W. is also a great composer. A large part of my act consisted of songs that he had written. Although all of his songs were quite beautiful, looking back, I think it was a mistake not singing songs that one's public is more familiar with.

The first night show went best. Many of my friends from work, John, and his mother, Helen, showed up. John C. sent me a dozen red roses for good luck, which I had placed neatly on the piano. I was a bit nervous at first but became more and more relaxed as the show went on. Most of my songs seemed to go over nicely, and I did not forget one lyric. All of the attendees seemed to enjoy it.

The second night's audience was a bit of a challenge. One lady, and I use the term lady loosely, was exceptionally loud and rowdy. I did my best and dealt with the situation as best I could. The rest of the audience tried their best to get her to "shut the hell up" but without much success. I would be singing a serious ballad and this drunken diva would be yelling her brains out!

To top that off, things were also a bit tense between Mr. W. and me that evening. For just before I was to go onstage, he hands me an unexpected surprise bill for his services. I know that being a pianist is his life's work, but the way he presented it, I found most disturbing. It's like buying a car and being told of the amount of bill at the signing. Whatever! At least I had my cabaret moment.

Tru starring Robert Morse, is a major success this year. *Tru*, naturally, was about the life of the great Truman Capote. I thought Mr. Morse was brilliant, and I sent him a fan letter. In my letter I wrote, *"Dear Mr. Morse, being an avid patron of the theater, I have always regretted not seeing Sir Laurence Olivier in person. After seeing your performance in* Tru, *I have no regrets."* I got a lovely thank-you note from him.

John will quit his job at Lord & Taylor at the end of the year after twenty-two glorious years. He just does not want to work there anymore because of its new management. He knew the store when it was at its peak.

This, sadly, was also the year Lucille Ball died. What a multitalented performer! She could do it all. I never tire of *I Love Lucy*. I still refuse to believe that they did not really take the Constitution to Europe. I am sorry I never got the chance to see her in person. I know this might sound a bit crazy, but for years, at night, I have always included Lucy, Ricky, Fred, and Ethel in my prayers. Those four certainly gave me a hell of a lot more happiness and laughs than many in my circle have.

1990

ONE SINGULAR SENSATION

A Chorus Line at the Shubert will close on April 28 after 6,137 performances. That is a pretty good run to say the least. I remember how it was next to impossible obtaining tickets for it during its first year. I was lucky enough to have gotten tickets. A few days before I was to see it, though, there was a death in my family and I had to fly to Dallas for the funeral. I went to the Shubert the day before my flight to see if anyone would care to buy my tickets. Are you kidding? The couple I sold them to was practically kissing me, feeling so lucky and excited to have them. I think I am still on their Christmas list. I will, eventually, get to see the show another time, which was magical.

I will still be doing my extra work in soaps this year when time permits. "One Life" will call me on and off all year. I just wish I could get a speaking part.

 BFT is planning to move uptown now. Will I still be able to say I work on Wall Street? I guess not. There is talk that we will be on Madison Avenue in the fifties. I guess I will have to get used to the subway again. Is that rude or what!

I was anxiously awaiting the end of December when I heard the Doyle Auction Gallery was auctioning off Rex Harrison's estate on December 13. I just had to own property that once belonged to the original Henry Higgins! I mean, really!

Unfortunately, something far more serious would occur in December. My beloved *friend* Louis Maniscalco will die from AIDS. I was aware that he had been sick with that terrible disease for more than a year. I just hoped and prayed that he would be one of the ones to beat it. I am beyond sick about his passing. I was so close with Louis. He was a very special person in my life, and I just cannot believe that he is gone. I loved Louis Maniscalco! The funeral will be on December 13.

I took a train to the vicinity of Yonkers and then took a cab to the funeral parlor. As is usually the case, I was seeing friends there whom I had not seen for quite some time. They were all just as heartbroken. We comforted each other as best we could. I kissed and caressed his crying mother. We were all in despair. I just cannot believe that Louis is gone.

I decided to take a taxi back. I just did not feel like going through the "sometimes agony" of the subway. On the way home, and I swear I did not plan this, the cab went right by the Doyle Gallery. I glanced at my watch and I figured the Rex Harrison auction was probably over, but I could go in and just check it out anyway. I asked the cab to stop, paid the driver, and proceeded to the gallery. The auction was not completely over, but there were only one or two items left unsold. One of the items was a blue sport coat. I quickly went to the front desk, applied for a number, and started bidding on the coat. Happily, I walked away with Rex Harrison's jacket. Louis would have wanted me to have it.

Tyne Daly was starring in *Gypsy*, this year. She was excellent! Stanley Hura, a good friend of John's and mine, took us to see it. *Gypsy* is such a great musical always revived on Broadway. (Moreover, I am still having coffee in its lyricist's kitchen.)

In July, Zsa Zsa Gabor will go to jail for three days after slapping a cop. Damn! What that does to my dinner plans!

1991

NYC MARATHON

Well, I am an uptown man now, at least work-wise. The move was really no big deal. The commute is a bit of a pain, but the good far outweighs the bad. Now I can have lunch every day at the Waldorf's Oscars. Their rice pudding is the best! Now it's *Breakfast at Tiffany's* and *Lunch at Oscars*. I can also pop over to Louis's more often, for Forty-Ninth Street is practically next door to my job. John and I will now be having dinner at the Mayfair much more often. Life is looking good!

I still check out *Variety* and all the trade papers daily. Once an actor, always an actor! I make note of some open calls in the Broadway vicinity. Open calls are good in that you can get into those difficult auditions that are solely for Actors Equity. The number of actors showing up for open calls is mind-boggling, though. Enough show up for mere auditions making open calls a real cattle call. At least I am in AFTRA now. I wish I could also get into SAG. Screen Actors Guild also seems a bit difficult getting into. (Years later SAG and AFTRA will merge and my problems solved.) I will always keep my membership alive, whatever amount of work obtained. I do attend a few of the open calls noted. Rejection! Rejection! Rejection!

The Will Rogers Follies is the hit musical this year. I will take my good friend Sunny to see it one evening. We both loved it! What a wonderful show! Comden and Green are amazing. Their music and lyrics, as always, are stupendous! They have given Broadway and the world so many hit shows. Keith Carradine and Dee Hoty were both amazing! You can't beat Tommy Tune's choreography.

Off Broadway also gave us the wonderful revue of Kander and Ebb music *And the World Goes Round*. Susan Strohman creates the outstanding choreography. I will go and see it several times. The songs are all so great. I am surprised that it never makes it to Broadway.

It is another summer in the Hamptons. The Bay Street Theater will open in Sag Harbor. It was founded by Sybil Burton (Richard's first wife), Emma Walton Hamilton (Julie Andrews's daughter), and Stephen Hamilton (Emma's husband). It will prove to be a great success. We will meet many a fascinating person there and see many a great show. I will be a big supporter of Bay Street in all the years to come.

I make up my mind. This will be the year I run the New York City marathon. I have been running my five miles a day for so long now. What is another twenty to add to that? It will be a cinch. The actual event is not until November 3, so I have quite a lot of time to train for it. I send in my application early in the summer to make sure I am accepted. With the thousands applying, there is really no guarantee, but happily, I am accepted and I have my place. I attempt to add a few more miles to my running each month in preparation.

November 3 arrives and it is marathon time. I am so excited! I wake up early, shave, shower, put on my new pair of running shoes, grab the subway train, and it is off to the starting point. Hundreds and hundreds of people are bunched together and all filled with excitement. It is hard to believe, but even with that number of people, I see a few friends. They are as excited as I am. The first bridge we run across is, actually, two bridge levels. All first-year runners are to run on the lower level. A friend fills me in and tells me that the higher level is narrower than

John Strangi

the bottom level and that I should try to run in the middle of the bridge. I ask him why. He tells me that because of all the water that everyone has been drinking, many runners relieve themselves on the sides of the bridge, causing a "golden shower" to downpour on the lower bridge. It's too bad I didn't bring my umbrella.

Starting time finally arrives and we are off. I approach the lower bridge. My friend was not kidding. I am soon "singing in the rain," but I survive. Shoulder to shoulder I travel mile after mile. I am filled with excitement. The many crowds and crowds of well-wishers we pass on the streets cheer us. I try to keep my pace borough after borough. We cross the Fifty-Ninth Street Bridge that is pretty much the halfway point. I have not lost my steam yet. I am filled with determination. I have to finish no matter what. Three hours into the race, I approach Fifth Avenue. I know I can finish! It approaches four hours and I am now in Central Park ready to near the finish line near Tavern on the Green. I cross the finish line, clocking in at four hours, thirty-three minutes, and fifty seconds. Out of pure exhaustion I actually cry along with the others. It is the release we all need. John and a couple of my other friends were waiting for me at the finish line. "I did it!" I am so proud of myself. I ran the New York City marathon! This is beyond cool!

We celebrated that evening with our friends Carol Rosenwald and Anne Greenburg at the Mayfair. Anne is a lovely woman that Carol introduced to us. Carol has always reminded us of a present-day Auntie Mame. We love her! That martini this evening tasted better than ever!

1992

CRAZY FOR YOU

This will be the year that the brilliant choreographer Susan Strohman will get her picture on the wall at Sardi's. Her musical *Crazy for You* opens to spectacular reviews. Along with best musical of the year, Ms. Strohman's choreography will also garnish a Tony.

Little Italy suffers a minor setback. John Gotti will go to jail for life. I guess that that's no more pizza parties for Mr. G.

John Strangi

I join a new gym uptown near my job and as always begin going religiously every morning. If I do not run those five miles every day, I feel lost. It gets my juices going.

I have made a new lunch buddy. During one of my afternoon lunches at the Waldorf's Oscar's, I meet a Frank Katusak. I introduce him to their rice pudding, which he too loves. We will be having a glass of wine at lunchtime each day for the next couple of years. For my birthday, one year he took me to La Grenouille, a restaurant that has been in NYC for years. It is gorgeous!

John and I will be having dinner uptown quite a lot now. The Mayfair will remain our favorite for years, remaining true to some of our favorites in the Village. That is the wonderful thing about NYC. There is a different restaurant on every block.

I will run the New York City marathon this year once again. This time, thank God, I began the race on the higher bridge. There were no raindrops falling on my head this go-around. I started the race with the same enthusiasm as last year, though halfway through I remember thinking "I proved myself last year. Why the hell am I going through all this again!" My finishing time was a little less than last year, but I still finished. I wonder if three is a charm. We shall see, but I rather doubt it.

Oh yes, and I will meet Arlene Francis this year, not running, but on my lunch break at work. As I am walking up Park Avenue, I see a woman standing in the front lobby of an apartment building between Fifty-Seventh and Fifty-Eighth Street. I approach her saying, "Ms. Francis, I have to tell you how much I have enjoyed you all of these years. You look as lovely as always." She replied, "Oh thank you, you've made my day."

I always enjoyed her, so much, on *What's My Line*. I remember, as a little boy, during their telecast from NYC, thinking someday I simply have to live in New York City. At least I have accomplished that.

1993

YOUNG AND FOOLISH

Well, this is the year I turn forty years of age. Boo! Hiss! Boo! Hiss! Oh, forty is not so old. I am still young and energetic. I can still dance the jig! I loved my thirties! I have matured and created a dynamite life for myself. I have not excelled in the theater, as I had hoped but there is still time. If I play Henry Higgins now, I will not have to wear half as much makeup.

Angels in America is the big hit play on Broadway this year. (When Mike Nichols directs the movie of "AIA" in 2002, I will work in it for several days). *Kiss of the Spider Woman* with Chita Rivera, is the smash musical this year.

This will be my final year of working for BFT. It was a good fourteen years, but I think it is time to broaden my horizons. April 30 will be my final day. As much as I sometimes dreaded going to work every day, my group of fellow workers have become like family, making it quite difficult saying good-bye. Does Johnny shed a tear or two? I think so. However, as they say in the theater, "A lifetime is a season and a season is a lifetime."

September 9 gets close, and I decide I would like to do something special for this landmark birthday. For my fortieth, John and I will be at the Hotel Metropole in Venice, Italy. I have booked it for

ten days. We have both been to Italy before but never with each other and never been to Venice. It sounds like fun.

Our ten days were beyond fun. They were glorious! Venice was everything I thought it would be and more. We did all the tourist things exploring every inch. One day we would go to the legendary area where they hand make glasses. There was a scene in the movie *Summertime* with Katharine Hepburn where during her stay in Venice, she buys a

beautiful red goblet. I set out to find a copy of that exact red goblet. I succeed. I find an exact replica. I have it to this day. Simply roaming the streets of Venice is pure magic. Every street corner is like a beautiful picture from a storybook. The only thing that we found a bit disappointing, strangely enough, was the food. It was becoming a bit of chore to find

John Castagna

John Strangi

a good Italian meal. Maybe it is the way we are accustomed to the Americanization of everything that made our task difficult. I don't know. On my birthday we dined at Harry's Bar, which was also a disappointment culinary-wise, but it was fun just going to such a legendary establishment. One evening we took a boat to the Hotel Cipriani on Giudecca Island. Now that is a gorgeous hotel! If I have another Italian venture in the future, I would like to stay at this hotel.

Back home, my brother Albert and his partner Greg Grey will pay us a visit toward the end of the year. We have such a grand time showing them all the sights. They loved going to top of Rockefeller Center and having cocktails in the Rainbow Room. The Rainbow Room is always a hit with its spectacular view. We would also treat them to the Rockettes at Radio City Music Hall. They always put on the best of shows. They, too, adored Sardi's! Of course, that goes without saying. We always have the best time with them!

Albert is about eight years older than I am, but we could not have been closer growing up. Those early years were such happy times. I was a mess when he went away to college. I must have cried for weeks.

Greg Grey, Albert Strangi, John Castagna, John Strangi

1994

IT'S NOT WHERE YOU START
IT'S WHERE YOU FINISH

John and I decide that this year we will move uptown. I have grown fond up uptown and cannot think of a better place to live. We researched everywhere looking from Washington Square to Sutton Place. We found a few in Sutton Place that we really liked, but after all was said and done we chose the Landmark at 300 East Fifty-Ninth Street. Our friend Jeremiah lives in that same building. We found an ideal one-and-a-half bedroom on the twentieth floor. I loved it! Each window looked onto New York City's colossal skyline. We discovered that the more reasonably priced apartments in some buildings had a higher monthly maintenance whereas the more expensive ones had a lower maintenance. Ours would cost $150,000 with a monthly maintenance of $2,000. I will be paying cash and will insist that John's name, too, be included on the lease. We hope to move in at the end of the year. We are not on Fifth Avenue yet, but this ain't bad.

Speaking of Fifth Avenue, this was the year that Jacqueline Kennedy Onassis dies. Mrs. Onassis passed away on May 19. What a tragedy! She was such a legend. I was never lucky enough to run into her in the city. My only semi-contact with the lady, was my being at Love Field Airport in Dallas on November 22, 1963. My brother Albert and I were among the thousands to meet their plane. On the day of her death, I walked to her apartment at 1040 Fifth Avenue and laid a small bouquet of red roses by the apartment's entrance. There were quite a number of sentiments of the same already there. NYC loved their Jackie!

The end of the year was quite emotional for John and me, to say the least. It was a weekend in October at Jeremiah's house, in the Hamptons, that I received a call that my father had died.

I immediately called for a bus to take me back to the city. When I arrived in the city, I called the airport and made flight arrangements for the following day. I would be leaving for Dallas early in the morning. I arrive in Dallas early the following day. I will be staying at Mother's in Dallas. Going home to my mother's beautiful face always brings a smile to mine. I have the best and most loving mother in the world!

The funeral is set for the following day. My brother, Albert, picks me up around eleven o'clock. He will be driving me, my sister Jeanne, and his partner/mate Greg Grey there for the services, which will be taking place at one in Waco. Family and friends met us at the church. I see so many faces I have not seen for years. After my parents were divorced, I saw very little of the Strangi side of my family, so recognizing my relatives was a bit of a chore. A funeral is a funeral is a funeral. Who likes them and if you do there's something wrong with you. As funerals go, I think Dad's was pleasant. I always hate seeing an open coffin, as I do not like having that picture being my last memory. Such is life, or should I say, such is death. After the customary after-funeral get-together, we headed back to Dallas. I remember most of us being rather quiet in the car.

With my parents becoming separated when I was ten years old and being divorced when I was thirteen, I hardly really knew my father at all. I regret that very much. He was a good father in his own way and what a successful businessman! He had a seventh-grade education and would go on to create multimillion dollar businesses. He had the Midas touch. (I never had the Midas touch, but I think I touched Midas once or twice.) I greatly admired Dad's genius.

After a few more lovely days with my mother, I head back to New York. It will be nice getting back. I hope that life will get back to normal and remain that way for a while.

Our friend Jeremiah's birthday is in October, and our friend Marge Shushan is planning a big party for him about ten days after my return. Marge and Jeremiah have been best friends for a million years. She is one of New York City's most successful interior decorators. Her lovely apartment is proof of that. She lives in the beautiful Museum Towers on the same street as MOMA. John and I are both planning on attending when John gets a call from his mother complaining about some ailment. We are prone to her false alarms on occasion, but we must be sure. We are not thinking it is anything serious, but John says he will go to her apartment and make sure all is okay anyway. I offer to go with him, but he tells me to go ahead and go to the party and that he would join us later when he can.

I arrive at the party at eight. The party is as festive as one would expect. I know most of the attendees. They are all my friends. Nine o'clock arrives and no John. Nine thirty approaches and no John! It is now ten o'clock and still no John. I call home several times and do not get any answer. I do not know what is going on. Why has John not answered my calls?

I leave the party and arrive at our apartment building at about ten thirty. Upon my arrival, I see John pacing in front of the building's courtyard. I run up to him and ask him what is wrong. He turns to me, face ashen, and says, "Mother died." I cannot believe it. In each other's arms, we break down crying. We are both in a state of shock. This just cannot be real! That beautiful, loving lady is gone. We are crying for the next twenty-four hours. This just cannot be and only ten days after my father! John, understandably, remains in a daze and in a permanent state of disbelief.

Neither of us slept much during the night. We both awoke still in a daze. Slowly we tried to take care of the matters that need be. Calling up our friends, loved ones, and telling them the news and taking care of the necessary arrangements. We were both trying to stay as strong as we had to. All of our friends and loved ones were as stunned as us.

The funeral would be in a few days following the customary wake. Many people will show up for both. There was not a dry face at either. John would remain strong throughout, only because he had to. Family and friends were sobbing nonstop. I think everyone was still in a state of disbelief.

Helen was one of the most loving women I have met in my life. She radiated charm and class. Class is not something one can buy. You either have it, or you have not, and she had it in abundance. I will miss the many trips John and I would make to her apartment always greeted with kisses and open arms. She would always surprise us with a dinner, serving us with another of her outstanding

Italian meals. Her superb cooking would cause Julia Child to cheer. She would never send us home empty-handed, always providing us with an armful of supplies for our refrigerator. It was all done with supreme love. Everything she did was with love. "You'll always be with us, Helen."

One day later another friend of ours, Rubin, will die of AIDS. Rubin had been John's friend much longer, but that does not make his passing any less painful to me. He was a lovely person and missed oh so much. They say that these things happen in threes. Unfortunately, it is staying true to form this time. I hope the coming months will be more peaceful and much less eventful.

Life must go on.

It is perhaps a good thing that before all of our recent unhappiness we had already signed the new lease on our apartment. Starting a brand-new chapter might turn out to be the best medicine. December 1 will be our moving day.

John's birthday is November 22. We invited Carol and Jeremiah to celebrate with us. I surprised John and rented a limousine for the evening. After picking us up downtown, it proceeded to pick up Carol and Jeremiah. We did not want to leave Jeremiah's without first taking a peek at our new apartment. The four of us take an elevator to the twentieth floor. *Drum roll!* The apartment is gorgeous. It is Carol's first time seeing it, and she thinks it's marvelous.

John Strangi, Carol Rosenwald, John Castagna

From the apartment, we have the limousine first drop us off at the Café Pierre for cocktails. Café Pierre has also become one of my favorite watering holes. From there we are taken to the Mayfair for dinner. Dinner at the Mayfair is always a pleasure. They surprise John with a birthday cake as well. After dinner, the limo takes Carol and Jeremiah home. With another birthday surprise up my sleeve, I have the limousine drop John and I off at the Waldorf Astoria where I have reserved a room for a few days. It is the end to a perfect evening. *Happy birthday to you!*

The next week is devoted much to packing. Our move is in just a little over a week. I had forgotten how much I hate moving, but this is a definite move up, so it is okay. Hell, it is a million times better than okay. The move is a real dream. Alleluia!

"Light the candles, it's today!" Moving day arrives and we are so excited. The moving men arrive around nine in the morning, and after a few hours we are on our way. We arrive to Fifty-Ninth Street at twelve. The movers have at it and in a couple of hours we are settled. Everything went by without a hitch except for a very large painting we have over our living room sofa. It is so large that it would not fit in the elevator. Fortunately, the building's manager will allow it placed on top of the elevator making its move possible. (When we move, ten years later, the building's new manager will not allow said solution, making it necessary for the movers and me to carry the picture down twenty flights of stairs.) Boxes and boxes surround us, waiting to be unpacked, but we could not be happier. With the exhaustion of the move, we decide that today we would only unpack the bare necessities.

Dinnertime arrives, and at eight o'clock, it is off to the Mayfair. We celebrate our new abode. All of our friends and drinking pals are so happy for us. It is the beginning of another new and exciting chapter.

1995

MONEY MAKES THE WORLD GO ROUND

You guessed it. I inherited quite a lot from Dad. So much so that I thought I was set for life. That remains to be seen, and so begins my money madness.

The apartment is shaping up fine. One of the first things we decide on doing is having some decorative wallpaper and marble floors put in both bathrooms. Throughout my many years of NYC living, I have become aware that in most New York apartments the bathroom seems to be the one room that people tend not to fix up. I intend to change that. The marble that we decide on is gorgeous. We, actually, should have had it done before the move because they tell us that the marble dust, which occurs during the remodeling, can be murder to one's furniture. We will manage. We do manage, and in a few weeks, the bathrooms are ready for *House Beautiful*. They both look gorgeous. In our one-and-a-half bedroom, I decide to make the half my office. The half is just outside of the kitchen overlooking Fifty-Eighth Street. Every day I'm blown away with our magnificent view of the city's skyscrapers. Our apartment is a corner, so we have outstanding views from all sides.

Victor Victoria, starring Julie Andrews, opens this year. I grabbed seats for it as soon as possible. I purchased six tickets, one each for John and me as well as for four friends. Well, as fate would have it, I unfortunately came down with the flu, making it impossible for me to go. I insisted to my friends that they go ahead and see it. They loved it, especially Carol.

John and I would see it a week or so later. I loved it! I will end up seeing it ten times. Ms. Andrews can do no wrong! The reviews are mixed, but I think it is exceptional.

One of my hobbies is dabbling in caricatures. I always thought of Al Hirschfeld as being the greatest ever. He has been drawing them of celebrities for years and is without question the best. The Margot Feiden Gallery on Madison Avenue displays his work. One weekend I was attending a special showing of his work. As I hopped on the elevator for the exhibition, a lady follows me in. It is none other than Ms. Helen Hayes. I practically fell over! I told her how much I had always admired her, loved her work, and that she was the best. She told me I was too kind. Ms. Hayes and I approached Mr. Hirschfield together. Apparently he and Ms. Hayes were well acquainted, which was no surprise. I introduced myself and told him how much I had always admired him. He autographed a postcard for me and shook my hand. He was charming.

Anyway, back to my hobby, Mr. Hirschfeld's caricatures appeared in the *New York Times* weekly. From the small drawing he did of *Victor Victoria*, I drew a large one of Ms. Andrews and Tony Roberts, her costar. One evening I left it at the stage door for her and several weeks later received an autographed thank-you note from Julie, which I have to this day.

I will take my very good friend, Josephine Franc, to see *Victor* next. I do not believe she is as big of a Julie Andrews fan as I am, but of course, who could match my deep adoration? Josephine has had a terrific job at CBS for many years. Josephine adores the show! This is my fourth time seeing it.

This summer, John and I will rent a charming house in South Hampton. Some friends of ours had rented it previously, so we knew what a charmer it was. My only complaint was that its only bedroom was upstairs on the second floor and its only bathroom was downstairs on the first floor. Going down the staircase after a few drinks was murder!

We threw one big party our first month, and it was a big success. Edward Albee showed up with his partner Jonathan Thomas. Jeremiah whispered to us not to be disturbed if Edward does not stay long because he hates parties. Well, he loved ours because he stayed to the end, which was well after one in the morning.

This years Tony Awards were a big disappointment. *Victor Victoria* will receive only one nomination that being Julie Andrews for best actress. Julie Andrews will refuse her nomination for *VV* as it was the only single nomination awarded to the show. I commend her for her action, but she more than deserved that award. Her performance was flawless. I will never understand it not being nominated for anything else. Rob Marshall's choreography was exceptional, and Blake Edward's direction was phenomenal. Sometimes there appears to be just no justice.

My darling Josephine Franc invites Linda Zecchino and me to join her at the Grammy Awards. CBS gave her some dynamite tickets. I had never been to that awards show before, and it was exciting. Much of the music was not up to my taste, but it was fun being there all the same.

John Strangi, Gloria Sacchi   Debra Mellman, John Castagna

Two lovely girls move in the apartment next to us, Gloria Sacchi and Debra Melman. Debra has a most successful job in advertising, and Gloria is vice president of a highly regarded real estate firm. They are both extremely attractive and sweethearts. Our lasting friendships are immediately set in stone.

1996

OH, JACKIE O'

September 30 is the day that I will own a house in the Hamptons. John and I will search in and around for several weeks finally discovering the winner in East Hampton. It is in a development of townhouses on Gingerbread Lane. It is a lovely two-story. The final asking price is $260,000, which I obtain a mortgage for. I regret obtaining it with a mortgage. I feel like it is just money thrown away. However, there is no use looking back, I guess.

Julie Andrews and Blake Edwards also own in the Hamptons. The hills are alive! I swear I am not stalking Ms. Andrews! We both possess the Hamptons bug.

We have begun going to many benefits in New York City as well as the Hamptons. One that we have attended for several years is the South Hampton Fresh Air Fund. It is to benefit disabled children. It takes place in May this year. We arrive for the event around 7:00 p.m. There is quite a good turnout this year. There are so many familiar faces. It looks like an enjoyable evening is in store. I order a glass of champagne, mingle madly, and stroll into the room to take a peek at the silent auction.

After eyeing and thumbing through several items, I decide to place a bid on two of them. My first bid is for a backstage tour of Broadway's *Victor Victoria*. I place a bid of $500. The next item to get my attention is a round of golf with Matt Lauer of the *Today Show*. The *Today Show* had always been one of my favorites, and I heard that Mr. Lauer might be taking over the position of coanchor early next year. I place a bid of $500 on this as well. With so many people attending this event, I really did not think I had the slightest chance of winning, especially with it being a silent auction, but who knows? Enter more mingling, more champagne, and more rubbing elbows.

One of the most celebrated people attending, whom I always see at this event, is a Mr. Donald Brooks. He has been a highly successful artist and fashion designer for years, his designs fought for among all the great department stores as well as being head costume designer for some mammoth movie productions. Among the movies he has designed for was 1968's *Star,* starring Julie Andrews. Many benefits ago he would comment to me that he would one day give me one of his designs from *Star.* Sadly, that was never meant to be, but in later years I would snatch one from one of the many auctions I attend.

Ten o'clock approaches and I am full of champagne and, frankly, all mingled out. It is homeward bound. We hop into my 1979 Jaguar, another recent buy, and hurry home. Eleven o'clock approaches and it is off to bed. What a nice evening!

I wake up around nine o'clock and stagger to the kitchen to make coffee. My days cannot begin in any way, shape, or form without my two or three cups of coffee. Hats off to java! I go into the living room and begin reading the Sunday paper. The *New York Times* is so immense; it takes you until Sunday of next week to finish it. After about two to three hours of reading the latest gossip and news, I retire to the bedroom for a short nap. I am about to doze off when the phone rings. I stagger to the phone and answer it.

It is the South Hampton Fresh Air Fund calling, informing me that I won both the *Victor Victoria* tour and golf game with Matt Lauer.

Reality creeps in. I have never played golf before in my life! We must stay calm and get a grip. Maybe Matt would just agree to have lunch or something, or perhaps I could tell him that I twisted my ankle. What am I to do? What am I to do? I like the ankle thing, much. Okay, let us get serious here. I probably have a month or two before our game. I could take lessons each week and be another Arnold Palmer in no time. Yeah, that is it! Problem solved!

I search the yellow pages and discover that Chelsea Piers, in Manhattan, gives golf lessons every day. This is cool! Where there is a will, there is a way! I place a call and arrange for my first lesson Monday at twelve noon. Oh, wait! I will have to buy a set of clubs first. I call and change my appointment to three. That should give me plenty of time to buy all the needed gear. Okay! This is cool. I have everything under control. Everything will work out. I will take complete charge tomorrow morning.

MONDAY–FIRST GOLF LESSON

It is another beautiful sunny morning in the Hamptons. I wake up around 7:00 a.m., and after a quick doughnut and coffee, John and I head for the Big Apple. The traffic on the LIE can be treacherous, but thankfully, most of the Hampton crowd returned to their NYC abode Sunday evening, making our drive less difficult. It takes us around two and a half hours to get home. I am settled back into the apartment around eleven. Okay, now it is operation Golf Game.

I scrounge for the yellow pages and, after a brief search, discover them at the bottom of my coat closet. I look under *G* (for you know what). There are so many golf shops! Who would have thought? The winner is one on East Forty-Seventh Street. I liked its ad best. I hop in a cab and venture off to the world of golf.

The cab drops me off in record time. I enter the store. I have never seen so many golf clubs my entire life! Wow! Not knowing a good golf club from a good baseball bat, I ask a salesman for assistance. Wise move, John. I explain to him that I am an amateur and that I really do not know a good golf club from a bad one. He steers me onto a nice set, followed by a pair of gloves, shoes, and balls. I mean, it is all or nothing, right? The grand total is $1,061.50. This is no big deal. I am feeling more professional with each second.

Three o'clock arrives and it is off to the Chelsea Piers for my first golf lesson. I arrive about two thirty clubs in hand and proceed to their main office to sign up for my lessons. A month of private lessons will amount to about $500. I go into the locker room and change into my golf attire. I then meet Jim, my golf instructor. He is about my age and seems nice enough. I quickly explain to him my

Matt Lauer saga. He seems rather amused and assures me we can tackle it together. Off we go to the arena to begin my hitting of golf balls into their far-off net.

Jim begins my lesson by instructing me on the proper stance I am to have. This is not hard. I have always been a great stander. Then I am, naturally, taught the correct swing. Swing 1! Swing 2! Swing 3! Hey, this is a cinch! Swing 4! Swing 5! Swing 6! Now my swing seems okay if you overlook my missing swing 4 and swing 6. This is no big deal! I shall overcome! I shall succeed! Swing 30! Swing 31! Swing 32! I could use a martini about now. Only I digress. My swing has lost its zing. I seem to be missing the ball more often than hitting it. Damn! I take a breather for five minutes.

Golf seems a bit harder than I imagined, and it should not be. I go to the gym every day. I am in the best of shape. I take my Flintstone's vitamins! I eat my spinach! Okay, let us take hold here. Let us get a grip, literally.

Swing 33! Swing 34! Swing 35! Swing 36! My snazzy green golf shirt looks like I just swam the English Channel! Swing 51! Swing 52! Swing 53! Martini, anyone?

During all this, naturally, Jim has done his best to try to help me with my lopsided swing and lopsided stance. He has proved a patient pro throughout. My hour golf lesson is almost up. Seriously, I think I did okay for my first time. Three days a week for the next two months should provide a happy ending. I hope.

Judging by my first day, I find golf a lot more strenuous than I imagined. My aching right arm is proof. Swing after swing after swing! It is exhausting! Maybe I just have to get used to it. When it all becomes second nature to me, perhaps it will flow like the tide. Well, it was a rough tide today. That is for sure! Those pros make it look so much easier. "Shame on you, pros!"

I have always been a bit of a perfectionist trying to be the best at whatever I do. Maybe I should give myself a report card each day. Today I will give myself a D. Too bad D does not stand for *Divine*.

Where the hell is that martini?

WEDNESDAY–SECOND GOLF LESSON

It is rather a gloomy Wednesday, overcast and a bit rainy, but I still prepare for my 3:00 p.m. golf lesson with the required optimism and gusto. I will lick this today! I feel it!

After my arrival, like yesterday, we spend the first thirty minutes focusing on my stance and posture. "Proper stance and proper posture enables a golfer to be perfectly poised throughout the swing." Did I say that? "The feet should be set apart the width of the shoulders." "The right foot is at a right angle to the line of flight, and the left foot is turned out a quarter of a turn to the left." "Keep the elbows and arms as close together as possible throughout the entire swing." "Bend your knees from the thighs down." "Legs must be supple, but at the same time must have live tension." "Enough already!"

Just shoot me! Please? I try my best to get all of my body parts to behave, as requested. I do okay but am thoroughly frustrated. The more I try, the more tense I get, which naturally produces the wrong result. I ask for a five-minute breather. Request granted! As I am seated on the nearest bench, I notice a ten-year-old kid approaching the driving range next to me. He proceeds to hit one ball after another, never missing. I hate this young child! I am not amused! I glare at this innocent victim. This tiny tot is a miniature Arnold Palmer. Fore!

Now that I have supposedly mastered the proper stance, it is time to hit a few balls. That tiny tot is in the corner of my eyes the entire time. I still do not like the infant much, but since my swing seems a bit better, I will take him off my hit list.

After about fifteen minutes, I ask for another breather. It really is exhausting hitting those damned balls nonstop. It really is! Who would have thought?

My day ends and Mr. Perfectionist is still not pleased. However, today I award myself a C. My grade should be better just for not getting violent with that kid.

FRIDAY–THIRD GOLF LESSON

I must be a glutton for punishment. Perhaps today will be a major success. Who am I kidding?

Once again, we begin our day going over the correct posture: head bent, knees pointed in, right foot perpendicular to the line. I feel like a mannequin in a Macy's shop window. No, let's make that Bergdorf Goodman.

Jim thinks it would be a good idea to focus mainly on hitting the balls today. Okay, I am all for that. "That sounds good to me." My swing seems a bit better today, and I seem to be hitting the ball better and more often. "Hail Mary, full of Grace, the Lord is with thee." My confidence is back! Oh, wait! How can it be back when it never was? It seems to be temporarily with me anyway.

I give myself a B- for the day. Things are looking up.

I stop off at Sardi's on the way home and celebrate with a martini. Actually, it is two martinis, or was it three?

During my second martini, I was thinking maybe I should change my golf lessons from three a week to two. Three interferes too much with my time in the Hamptons. I will do it! I will ask for the change at my next lesson.

MONDAY–FOURTH GOLF LESSON

Mission accomplished! I arrived for my lesson today around 2:00 p.m. immediately requesting a visit to the business office. I explained my "time in the Hamptons" predicament, and the problem solved. After this week, I would switch to two lessons a week, on Tuesday and Thursday, each one being for an hour and a half.

It is lesson time! Today's lesson began with a review of last week's teachings. I felt as if I was a bit more comfortable with everything though I still missed my share of balls.

MONDAY–C- More of the same

WEDNESDAY–C- More of the same

FRIDAY–C- More of the same

It is too bad that C does not stand for *colossal*.

It would be redundant as well as boring to discuss all of my lessons for the entire two months. I became familiar with putting during the last weeks. I thought it, at least, might be a bit easier than the rest, but sadly, it was not. I was always so good at miniature golf! Show me to that windmill!

I also, one day, got a call from NBC telling me that our golf day was switched to October 1, giving me even more time to practice. They also mention that our twosome has become a foursome. Two other folks from NBC would be joining Matt and me. Just shoot me! Now I have to make a fool of myself in front of three people instead of only one. Matt also asked his secretary to ask me what my handicap is. It is as if I even have one. I just told her that I was not sure. I know that, in golf, a handicap is a low number, but I was not sure how low. I will just fake it!

The next few months I ran the gamut of emotions from *A* to *Z*. I would be confident one day and totally frustrated the next. I would try so hard on one day and then leave completely frustrated on the next. "I'm determined to lick this damn game!"

OCTOBER FIRST -D-DAY

The day has arrived at last. We will be playing our round of golf at the Stanwich Country Club in Greenwich Connecticut. Our golf date is October 2, so John and I arrive in Greenwich the evening before. I had never been to Greenwich before. It is gorgeous! We check into a quaint little hotel called the Homestead Inn.

With some free time to spare, I decide it might be a good idea to locate the country club today so that there will be little chance of my arriving late tomorrow. We are amazed and dumbfounded at all the mammoth mansions we pass. Hell, all those mansions are so large that each one could pass for a country club! Our search continues. After an hour and a half, we do locate the club. It is beautiful and the golf course is unbelievable. It goes on for miles. I guess that that's par for a golf course.

We then decide to take a drive into the village and explore the town, getting my mind off the game, or at least trying. Greenwich really could not be lovelier. It is an authentic storybook town, each block more picturesque than the next, with charming little shops. One expects Hansel and Gretel to come skipping down the streets any second.

After a few hours of exploring the many shops and boutiques, we head back to the inn and retire to our room. I decide to take a little catnap. I wake up feeling a bit groggy but arrange myself well enough to have dinner in the dining room that evening. We go downstairs where I immediately order a martini, very dry. Oh, yes! "How sweet it is." I then order two pork chops baked to perfection. This Arnold Palmer is feeling just fine. Feeling fine and dandy, we retire to the room. I ponder tomorrow. "What is going to happen? How will I play? Will I miss the ball? Will I make a fool of myself? Was this all a major mistake?" Tune in tomorrow, folks, for the answer. I go downstairs and order another martini to calm my nerves.

"Raindrops on roses and whiskers on kittens." I am afraid remembering my favorite things does not help this time. I have another martini. I recall that episode on *I Love Lucy* with Lucy and Ethel taught, incorrectly, how to play golf. Ricky and Fred teach them all these ridiculous rules where they will give up the game. Only that is make-believe, is it not, and this is the real thing!

I must be positive! Things could turn out fine. Who knows, maybe I will play so well tomorrow that I inquire about becoming a member of Stanwich. Matt and I could become regular golf buddies. Oops! I think I have gone back to make-believe.

OCTOBER 2

GOLF GAME

I wake up around eight o'clock feeling okay. Originally I thought I would have my coffee sent up to the room but decide to have breakfast downstairs in the dining room instead. Do they serve martinis this early? I feel like a light breakfast, possibly starting with cereal. I wonder if they have Wheaties. Hell, I need all the help I can get. After my cereal and toast, I retire back to my room. Tee time is scheduled for twelve noon, so I take my time preparing for our match. I lie on the bed for a bit, watching a bit of the news and weather. I pray for rain.

At 10:30 a.m., we set out for the club. John drops me off and I proceed to the front desk to inquire about the locker room's where-abouts. During my walk there, I am blown away by what an immense country club this is. It is enormous! I belonged to a country club growing up, but this one makes it look like a kiddy camp. I proceed to the locker room. It is your typical locker room with a locker here and a locker there. "A rose is a rose is a rose." I change into my golf ensemble and wait. I recite the Our Father and Hail Mary twice. At around a quarter to twelve, I leave the locker room for the golf course clubs in hand. I had even stuck a camera in my golf bag with hopes of having a picture taken with Matt at the end. After about five min-utes, Matt drives up in a golf cart with the other two NBC executives and a caddy. To protect the innocent, I will refer to the other two NBC executives as Heckle and Jeckle. I am feeling rather nervous, but I try to remain cool.

Matt introduces himself to me, along with Heckle and Jeckle. They were all very welcoming, and especially Matt. Matt looks the same as he does on TV, though a bit thinner. We begin our match with the usual small talk.

"It's so nice to meet you."

"I have so been looking forward to this day."

"How long have you played golf?"

Matt has been playing golf since he was a little boy. That goes for Heckle and Jeckle as well. They all seem to be semipros. "Oh, woe is me!" This is not the time to tell them of my newness to the game. They will find out I'm a novice soon enough.

CURTAIN UP

HOLE 1* Guess who gets to go first. It is none other than yours truly. Thanks a lot! "Oh please, oh please, oh please, just let me hit the ball." Okay, here we go. I'm thinking left arm fully extended, right arm slightly bent, knees pointed in. I have got the proper stance! I think. I prepare to swing. Ready! Set! Go! I hit the ball! Yes, thank God, I did actually hit the ball. It was not the best of shots, but I did get the ball off the tee. My shot was a bit too far to the left, far away from the green, naturally.

Matt is next to tee off. "Fore!" What a shot! His ball almost hits the green, unlike mine. His shot went straight down the fairway. Our other two golf buddies were just as successful, naturally. One of their balls actually made it to the green. Is that rude or what!

It is time for my second shot. At least now that my ball is so far away from everyone else's no one will notice if I miss it or not. That is a good thing too because I did miss hitting it. In fact, it took me three swings to hit the damn ball. I am still not on the green, but that goes without saying. They all make it to the green in no time. I begin feeling frustrated, and embarrassed. I would like nothing better than to crawl in my golf bag and escape. After several more failed attempts, I finally make it to the green. It is putting time! All three of them score a par four. I make the hole after thirteen tries! Do you suppose that that number 13 is an omen? Time will tell.

HOLE 2* This hole appears to be a bit farther than the first, or perhaps I'm just hallucinating. I am number three to hit this time. Matt shot first followed by Heckle. Heckle made a heck of a shot, making it right on the green. Even in my madness, I can still recognize perfection. Now it is my turn. I gently place my ball on the tee and, after a quick prayer or two, have at it. Once again, my beloved ball went way off to the left. I make it to the green after about seven tries. "I have to concentrate! I have to focus!" I am feeling like such a fool! The three stooges all score par. Naturally. I make the hole after eleven tries. At least I scored better than the last one.

HOLE 3* Do you think that my golf buddies have figured out yet how much of a novice I am? I have a funny feeling they have. Matt sees my frustration and embarrassment. He tells me not to worry and not give my "less than sparkling performance" a second thought. "We don't have to keep score and can just play for fun." All right, I am willing to go that route. That sounds mighty fine to me! Perhaps that will make my playing a tiny bit better. The pressure might subside. Fat chance! This one was a hole in eight for me. "Ouch!"

HOLE 4* I know Matt said to just relax and have fun, but I am just not cool with that. I have always tried to be a perfectionist, and this is just turning out to be such a bummer. "Damn!" I go first this time. My shot was actually okay but nothing to write home about. They all make it to the green in no time and score their par. Twelve was my delightful total this time.

HOLE 5* As we tee up for the fifth hole, my eyes are drawn to one beautiful spectacle. No, it is not Raquel Welch. I notice, above, a dark rain cloud. Oh please, oh please, oh please let it rain! Let my misery end. Oh, dear God, please! "I promise to go to church every Sunday." I even thought I felt a drop or two. Sadly, the cloud does not deliver and it is time for another of my dynamite swings. I approach my ball, give it my best shot—only this turns out to be my worse shot yet. I was not sure where my ball landed. I think it landed in a different time zone. My caddy, who I am now ready to adopt, eventually finds it. I finish this one, a hole in thirteen. Can things get much worse? I bet they can.

HOLE 6* Is there a doctor in the house?

HOLE 7* What if Matt mentions this to Katie Couric? I'm ruined!

HOLE 8* "Hail Mary full of grace...

HOLE 9* I'm about ready to call 911, but I do make it through the ninth hole. This was a hole in eight and a half for Mr. Novice. I say a half because I kicked the ball at one point.

Matt suggests we take a break and go into the clubhouse for a bite to eat. I am thrilled with the idea! I first go into the locker room, splash a bit of water onto my face, trying to look presentable to all of the clubhouse cronies, and then make my entrance. We sit at a table by the window. I really don't have too much of an appetite, but I adjust. We all four order our Stanwich sandwich and have at it.

I am feeling like such a fool. I cannot stress enough how charming and understanding my three golf buddies were about my rotten playing. They could not have been nicer.

As we finished lunch I thought it best I decline on playing the second nine. I told them all what a pleasure it was meeting them all only I think best I depart. I am sure they were heartbroken.

Note: That camera I put in my golf bag, to have pictures taken with Matt, was never disturbed. After my rotten playing, I could not even go there. It is a shame too. I know Matt would have been happy to oblige. (If you are reading this book, Matt, you owe me one.)

I just felt so embarrassed. I could not even bring myself to watch *The Today Show* for months. I will call John to pick me up. I do not immediately tell him of my blunder but decide to fess up before we get to our hotel. He is more than sympathetic. Where's that martini!

OCTOBER 3

I am back to my apartment in Manhattan, still reeling in grief from my miserable golf game. I must rise above it! What about my other auction win? The *Victor Victoria* backstage tour is waiting for me. That should temporarily ease my many woes. Yes, let us take a shot at it. (What a bad choice of words!) Let us take a stab at it.

I search for my phone book, call the theater, and request to speak to the manager. I tell the man of my auction win and after checking his records he tells me that any evening next week would work out fine. We decide on the following Saturday.

SATURDAY

It is time for *Victor Victoria*. This will be my fifth time seeing it. Poor John, I have dragged him so many times to see the show.

We leave for the theater at 7:00 p.m. The show is at eight, but with NYC traffic, one has to play it safe. If I miss the overture of any show, my night is ruined, so I always prefer to arrive more than early. We arrive at seven thirty and the house seems relatively full. I am seated center orchestra, next to a rather overweight woman with a child. "Please may this child be a silent one." There should be complete silence during a show. Occasionally I will be unfortunate enough to sit by a talkative couple. Any unnecessary noise at all causes me to fume! It is the height of rudeness.

The show begins. There is that overture! Goose bumps! The first act is picture perfect as well as the rest of the show. That little child was a quiet one after all. It is another victory for *Victor*. After the majority of the crowd has left their seats, I shyly wander to the stage door and tell the doorman of my auction win. He shows me to a seat and calls the stage manager. The stage manager, Sheila, greets us and escorts us to center stage. She is very nice and is about my age. What a thrill to look across stage to those hundreds of seats filled night after night. Sheila then takes us to a computer that handles all the backstage magic. This computerized brain handles the lighting, scenery, etc. Of course, one does have to know the correct buttons to switch. Ain't life tough! We then hike upstairs to the dressing rooms. I see Julie's dressing room as well as her costars. Unless you are one of the featured stars, you usually have to share a dressing room. "Rude! I want my own!" I was hoping, by chance, that Ms. Andrews might stroll out of hers, but no such luck. However, I did touch her door.

Our tour ends. We head downstairs. I ask Sheila if I might walk on the stage once more. She gladly obliges. I go to center stage and have my final curtain call. Without sounding too dramatic, there really is something magical that one feels on a Broadway stage. That could apply to any stage for that matter, but especially on a Broadway one.

CURTAIN UP

My next big venture occurred during the summer. I had strolled into the Margo Feiden Gallery one day to admire Al Hirschfeld's work when an idea hit me. I summoned one of its employees and asked if one had to be a big, successful actor to have Mr. Hirschfeld do your caricature. I was told "No, he will do one for anyone," even an unemployed actor like myself. I inquired as to the price. It is close to $11,000. I really did not find that price too much when you consider one of the greatest artists/caricaturists in the world will be doing your picture. Sold!

I ask what the usual procedure is. I am told to first drop off several snapshots of myself, which I do during the coming week. I am then told that the actual sitting will be in his studio, at his townhouse, in two weeks.

My portrait day arrives. I am so excited! At twelve thirty, I hop in a cab and head to Mr. Hirschfeld's townhouse on Ninety-Fifth

Street. I approach the front door and ring the bell. The housekeeper meets me at the door, escorting me in. She shows me to a seat and informs Mr. Hirschfeld that I have arrived. It is your typical New York townhouse. I am betting he bought this one during the twenties or thirties. It reminds me of Ms. Hepburn's with the same sort of old furniture. The entire townhouse reminds me of Kate's. (We are on a first-name basis now, you know.) After about ten minutes, I am told that he is ready for me.

On their staircase, I see one of those electrical, movable chairs that can transport one up and down the staircase with ease. The housekeeper asks me if I would care to use the chair. I thank her but decline. "I'm still in my forties, toots!" I walk up the stairs to his studio, which is on the fourth floor. Mr. Hirschfeld sits in what looks like an old, comfortable barber's chair. He gets up and shakes my hand. I tell him how much of a thrill this is as well as how I have always been one of his biggest fans. He was charming. He thanked me and then told me where he would like me to sit for my picture.

I will be sitting in a chair about ten feet from his desk. He takes his seat once again in his barber's chair and reaches for his sketchpad. My sitting lasted around twenty-five minutes. He did two sketches of me, which I never saw.

My session is over. I thank him and proceed downstairs where I hail a cab. I cannot quit thinking about what just happened. "I'm going to be immortalized!" Is this cool or what?

I will receive the finished product in about a month. It will be twenty-seven inches by thirty-two inches framed. There are two "Nina's" in it. One is in one of my sideburns and the other in my hairline. It is so cool the way he always tries to put his daughter's name in his caricatures. The only thing about my caricature that I had semi-mixed feelings about was my hair. I know my hair was longer then, but he made it kind of afro/Whoopi Goldbergish. Caricatures are supposed to be an exaggeration of one's features, so I let it pass. Who am I to question a legend?

John Strangi

I will be running into Mr. Hirschfeld quite a lot the next few years. I will become a supporter and benefactor of many organizations of Mr. Hirschfeld's.

November 7 will be our next encounter. The Landmark Conservancy will be honoring a number of legends, Mr. Hirschfeld being one of them. He becomes a landmark with Brooke Astor, Peter Duchin, Mathilde Krim, Felix Rohatyn, and Liz Smith. The award ceremony will be in the grand ballroom at the Plaza. The evening's festivities will begin with cocktails in the Plaza's Frank Lloyd Wright suite.

John and I arrived in the Frank Lloyd Wright suite around six thirty. We were among the first. Only a few of the honorees were among this early gathering. As we are sipping our glass of champagne, the grandest dame of them all, Brook Astor, walks in. She is very elegant. She kisses us both and utters, "When do we get into the bed." There was a large bed in the center of the room. Considering we are in a hotel, I suppose that is to be expected. Thirty minutes later, it is Ms. Astor's turn to make a short speech. She meanders to a small stage in the room and delivers a charming speech. At its end, she utters, "It looks my assigned escort isn't here to walk me off." Brendan Gill, who was assigned to be her escort, had not arrived, so I rush to the small stage, take Ms. Astor's arm, and say "I'll be your escort, please allow me." I then proceed to walk her off the stage. She thanked me with another kiss on my cheek. It was such an unexpected thrill!

The award ceremony in the Grand Ballroom was so exciting. I waited for the right moment to go up to Mr. Hirschfeld and congratulate him. I uttered, "Remember me?" He replied, "Of course, and so good to see you." Carol Channing was among the many celebrities hovering around him. She looked great! Liz Smith was to give a very entertaining acceptance speech. What a delightful evening!

Another big happening this year was Sotheby's auction of the estate of Jacqueline Kennedy Onassis. It will take place April 23 to 26. I wanted so very much to get tickets for it, but such a venture was next to impossible. John and I were able to go to a preview of the items for sale but no tickets for the actual event.

So what am I to do? I will simply write in a few bids, and I will make exorbitant bids on everything where I surely will own at least one item of hers. I bid on a gilt-metal cross brooch and pendant cross necklace. A picture of Mrs. Onassis wearing the brooch is in the album. Then I bid on a pair of crème-ware candlesticks. A picture of President and Mrs. Kennedy with the candlesticks is also in the catalogue. An engraved silver waiter with initials JLB was my third choice, followed by a wooden olive-green wall bracket and an original copy of Noel Coward's

Present Indicative. I had no idea if I would be successful with any of my bids, but I gave it my best shot.

April 23, the first day of the auction, arrives and as I expected, the majority of Mrs. O's items are selling for a hundred times their estimated value. This mad buying will occur on every day of the auction. I give up hope. What chance have I now? *Such is life!*

A week later, I receive a call for Sotheby's. Maybe I did win something after all. I won something all right! I won every one of my bids! My exorbitant bids worked after all. I could have bought a house in Florida for what it all cost. Ouch! Money management is not one of my strong suits.

IS THERE A PSYCHIATRIST IN THE HOUSE?

Picture it: 851 Fifth Avenue–Penthouse of Dr. Marvin Orbach

Michele St. John

Dr. Marvin Orbach lives and works out of his gorgeous twenty-seventh-floor penthouse apartment.

DR. ORBACH: *Good afternoon, John. What is it exactly that you wished to discuss with me?*

JOHN: *Well, I have this obsession.*

DR. ORBACH: *We all have an obsession or two. What concerns you about yours?*

JOHN: *My obsession is with auctions. I just paid over one hundred thousand dollars to own something that once belonged to Jackie Kennedy Onassis. Well, actually, I won five items and their total estimate was under one thousand dollars.*

DR. ORBACH: *Yes, I think we could call that an obsession. What do you suppose makes you desire these items so greatly.*

JOHN: *You tell me! I mean, isn't that why I'm here? That money could have paid for a house in Florida.*

DR. ORBACH: *It could have paid for several houses.*

Mary Lou Emery

Jacqueline Kennedy Onassis

Gloria Sacchi

Jean Wood

Amy Arnold

Bennet

Joan Farrington

I place a call to my stockbroker in Washington and tell her to wire me the money. She is not pleased, but then it is my money, thank you very much. After the wiring is complete, and the check written, it is off to Sotheby's to pick up my loot.

John Strangi Randy Arnold

Carolyn Doyle

I arrive at Sotheby's on an early Friday morning. One by one, all of my "wins" handed to me. I am very excited. There was another man beside me picking up his merchandise as well. "I'll show you mine if you'll show me yours." We congratulated each other, one crazy New Yorker to another. I head back to Fifty-Ninth Street and show John my goodies. I know John thinks I am out of my mind, but he has learned to bite his tongue with regard to my fancies. John is impressed with the candlesticks. We find a striking place to dis-

Carol Rosenwald

play them in our living room. I place the jewelry on Bennett, my stuffed sheep. Bennett is thrilled.

It will become a regular routine of mine when we have guests to ask if he or she would like their picture taken wearing Jackie O's jewelry. My darling first cousin Randy Arnold visited often with her husband James. We always have the best time with them. Randy was one of the first to wear Jackie O's jewels. I think Jackie would be proud!

A funny little coincidence occurred about a month after the auction. I had joined a gym located two blocks down from me on Fifty-Seventh Street. I still preferred working out early in the morning, so 6:00 a.m. was my usual starting time. The gym was on the fourth floor of this apartment building. On this particular day, I approach the elevator at exactly 6:00 a.m. A woman, with that "just got out of bed" look, is standing next to the elevator. She comments,

"Oh, I'm so glad you're here. I hate riding in the elevator alone." I am thinking, "Okay, maybe this woman is just a bit claustrophobic or she is some bag lady planning to rob me in the elevator." With her standing next to me, I look more closely, and strangely enough, this woman, with no makeup, looks slightly familiar. When the elevator door opens on our floor, this mystery lady darts in front of me and heads straight for the reception desk to sign in. Standing behind her, I peak at her signature to see "Lee Radziwill," Jackie O's sister. I should have said, "Honey, your sister just cost me a hundred thousand dollars." I had seen her at benefits and functions in the past, but without her makeup on I just did not recognize her. During my workout, she did come out of the dressing room with her face on. Hat's off to Max Factor. We smiled at each other. I toyed with the idea of speaking to her but didn't. During the coming years, I will see quite a bit of Mrs. Radziwill in the Hamptons where she owns a spectacular house on the water. She is now married to the well-known Herbert Ross.

This year will also be the thirtieth anniversary of *Thoroughly Modern Millie*. There will be a big gala celebrating it on February 26. John had read it in the paper and brought it to my attention. I'm sure he knew he would be in major hot water if he didn't. I bought tickets for it immediately. I'll bet I still know half the dialogue by heart. Its proceeds will go to Broadway Cares, so I donated a hefty amount. Both of our names are listed in the programs.

First, in the theater district was the showing of the movie, followed by a reception at the Millennium. The theater was jam-packed with devoted fans and admirers. Carol Channing was the only star there from the original cast. She was great as always. We forgive Julie for not coming due to her *Victor Victoria* workload. Carol discussed the making of the movie as well as performing a number or two. She was super!

"Everything today is thoroughly." I am not thoroughly through with this year yet. The Russian Tea Room is closing, and they are having an auction in December. "Did someone say *auction*?" I have to own something from an establishment as well known as the Russian Tea Room! I mean it's a must.

Its auction will actually take place in the first floor of the Tea Room. It is a packed house, to say the least. I maneuver into the crowd and find a space to stand shoulder to shoulder with all. The auction begins. With so many people, at times, it is almost impossible to see its auction item. I manage to bid on a few small items at first. I manage to win a few cups and saucers as well as a small marble table. Then I hear the auctioneer say, "If you want a real piece of the Russian Tea Room, this item is for you." I raise my hand and place a bid. I am really not 100 percent sure what I am bidding on, but I continue with my bidding, winning this mystery item for $1,000.

The next day John and I proceed to the Tea Room to pick up my items. As expected, there are a number of people there doing the same. We collect my cups, saucers, and marble table. This is cool. We can easily fit all these into a cab. The marble table can go into the trunk. Oh, wait! We still have to collect my one-thousand-dollar "piece of the Russian Tea Room." Then it is off to their back room where I collect my final win, which is a large partition wall. I bought an entire wall! This is not cool. What am I going to do with this wall? It is gigantic!

In the center of this wall is a large logo of the Russian Tea Room. An idea comes to me. There are many carpenters here roaming around and taking care of the Tea Room's demise. Perhaps I could pay one of them to cut the logo from the wall. That would make a classic picture. I summon one of the carpenters and he agrees to do just that. I pay him $50 and he goes at it. The wall turns out to be a bit thicker than we imagined, so it takes a bit longer than we had imagined, but not without success. The carpenter presents me with my "carving" and all is well. I love happy endings!

The next day I take my "carving" to our local picture framer and request framing. Sold!

My auction madness continues when I hear of another biggie at Sotheby's.

DR. ORBACH: *Back so soon?*

JOHN: *I'm afraid so. There was another auction at Sotheby's.*

DR. ORBACH: *I hope you didn't buy another house in Florida?*

JOHN: *No, but I definitely could have used the money for a down payment on a boat. Oh, and I also bought a wall from the Russian Tea Room.*

DR. ORBACH: *A wall?*

JOHN: *Yes, but I didn't take the entire wall home. I had some carpenters cut out its insignia.*

DR. ORBACH: *Wise move!*

JOHN: *I am afraid I made a little damage at an auction house in Las Vegas as well.*

DR ORBACH: *What was your damage with them?*

JOHN: *Oh, I don't know. I think it is around ten thousand or so.*

DR. ORBACH: *As long as these purchases give you enjoyment.*

JOHN: *They do, but part of me says that it is just throwing money away. I have been spending so much lately. Oh, and I bought a house in East Hampton, only it is a mortgage. In addition, I had to purchase a car.*

DR. ORBACH: *What kind of car did you buy?*

JOHN: *A Mercedes Benz. I also bought a 1979 Jaguar. A fellow in the Hamptons was driving it around with a For Sale sign on it. It is so beautiful! It's an English white with red interior.*

DR ORBACH: *Excuse me, while I go to the bathroom.*

1997

LE JAZZ HOT

We will be spending quite a lot of time in the Hamptons this year. With neither of us working now, John and I can drive there during a weekday, avoiding all the weekend traffic. The weekend traffic is always horrific!

During one of our evenings out at a quaint little restaurant just on the outskirts of East Hampton, we became aware of a familiar face at a nearby table. The man looked like Michael Nouri, Julie Andrews's costar in *Victor Victoria*. It looked like him because it was him. Well, I just  had to go up to him and say something. I approached his  table and told him how crazy I was about the show and how great he is in it. He was very nice and in fact invited me to visit him backstage in his dressing room anytime. I said that would be great because I do have some friends visiting me from out of town next week, and they would love that. How nice of him to make such an offer!

Michele St. John was my visiting friend. She and her husband were here for a few days. Unfortunately, the evening we had tickets for *Victor*, Julie Andrews was not in it. Out of the many times I saw *VV*, this was the only time she did not play. I was sorry for Michele that Julie was not in it, but she still seemed to enjoy the show. As Michael had promised, we did get to go backstage to his dressing room and see him. Michele  loved that! Maybe that made up for Julie not being in the show. No, not quite, but it was still a thrill getting to visit backstage. Michael's dressing room was directly opposite Julie's. This was my seventh time seeing *Victor*.

Within a couple of weeks I will be seeing *Victor* again with a few friends and boldly ask to visit Michael backstage. I had hoped I was not coming off too pushy, but happily, Michael could not have been more welcoming.

To show my appreciation to Michael, I thought I would draw one of my Hirschfeld-like caricatures for him. I worked on it for several days. As a rule, I draw my caricatures in pencil, but this one I decided to do in ink. I actually think they look better in ink. I was very happy with the result and presented it to Michael at one of the evenings shows. He loved it!

Sadly, the unthinkable will happen this year. Julie Andrews will have surgery on her throat and during the operation will lose her beautiful singing voice. A Picasso destroyed! It is so hard to believe that that beautiful God-given voice that pleased millions for years and years is gone. A careless mistake by a surgeon is to blame. My heart goes out to her.

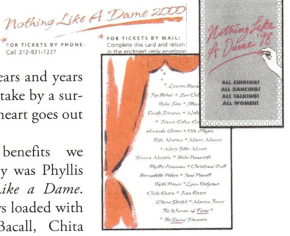

One of the benefits we began attending yearly was Phyllis Newman's *Nothing Like a Dame*. Each year it was always loaded with celebrities: Lauren Bacall, Chita Rivera, Elaine Stritch, and Joan Rivers, just to mention a few. It was always a fun evening. All of the celebrities would always put on a super show. It was always the biggest of musical extravaganzas.

1998

I'M JUST WILD ABOUT MARY

Sotheby's will be having an auction of the Duke and Duchess of Windsor this February. It was supposed to have taken place at an earlier time but, due to Princess Dianna's death, cancelled. I attended one of the many evenings and left with a lovely caricature of the Duchess.

My dream of finally meeting Julie Andrews, in person, will come true this year. One of our favorite haunts in East Hampton is an outstanding restaurant called Santa Fe. The owner, Kevin Boles, and all of his workers are super. We begin to think of them all as family. They have many loyal patrons. One of their loyalists is a fellow named Michael. Michael will eventually marry, our favorite waiter, Lynn.

Michael will become Julie Andrews's house boy for several years, driving her and Blake back and forth from the city as well as taking care of matters at their house. (Some guys have all the luck!)

Well, as fate would have it, on April 29, back in the city, I am walking across Forty-Second Street and I spot Michael standing in front of a Jeep. I utter, "Michael, what are you doing here," to which he replied, "John, come here, I want you to meet someone." He then introduces me to Blake Edwards seated in the Jeep. We say our hellos with a bit of small talk. I tell him how *Breakfast at Tiffany's* had always been one of my favorite movies. He was charming. Then Michael says "Wait five minutes and you can meet Julie." I am about to faint. Ms. Andrews was attending some function in a nearby recording studio.

Drum roll, please! Julie walks over looking as much like Mary Poppins as ever. Michael introduces me to her. I first say, "Ms. Andrews, I have been in love with you ever since *Mary Poppins*," to which she says, "Oh, thank you. It's so nice to meet you." We touch! I touched Julie Andrews! Life does not get much better than this.

Michael told her I had a house in the Hamptons and that we are neighbors. We talked a bit about life out there. I thanked her for the many hours of entertainment she had given me. I told her too that I had seen *Victor Victoria* nine times. She was the perfect lady, everything I thought she would be.

I did an Off-Broadway play this year called *Walk On, Walk On.* It was not much of a success. We rehearsed for a couple of weeks at a theater on the east side. We played a couple of weeks on the east side. We closed in a couple of weeks on the east side. With it being such a flop, my memory of it is rather limited. All I can say is that we should have changed its name to *Walk Off, Walk Off,* for that is exactly what most of our audiences did, only not soon enough. Sometimes things just do not work, and this was one of those times.

I should have taken some of my newfound wealth (which is shrinking) and auditioned for Julliard again, but I didn't. Instead, I took acting lessons in the Hamptons from Emma Walton and Steven Hamilton at Bay Street. They would give them for several summers. I enjoyed taking lessons from them and found them quite good. I, at auditions to this day, still use a monologue that Emma suggested for me. It's a piece from *Other People's Money.* How ironic!

My Henry Higgins was almost reborn. I had read that an Off-Broadway production of *My Fair Lady* was in the works and open auditions held on Broadway and Forty-Third Street. I had always hoped that one day I could play that part again. Unfortunately, at the start of the audition, I would learn that its run would interfere with a California trip that John and I had previously arranged for October. I thought I had read well and hoped that somehow my conflicting schedule would not be a problem. Either my schedule was a problem, or my audition stunk, for I would not hear back from the show's director. Damn!

We did have a nice time in Los Angeles. We traveled there with Jeremiah. Some good friends of his wanted to help him celebrate his birthday. His birthday party was great fun, and it was a real thrill meeting so many of his talented friends. The friend that gave us the greatest thrill was the legendary Tony Duquette. Tony was one of the entertainment world's best! His magnificent house was beyond thrilling. His house overflows with the magnificence of his talent. I had never seen anything so grand!

We were also, this year, invited to one of Edward Albee's Christmas parties. It was always at his gigantic loft apartment in downtown Manhattan. The list of celebrities there would go on for miles. Lauren Bacall, Elaine Stritch, and Kathleen Turner were among the many. It was charming the way Ms. Turner came up to us and introduced herself.

Jonathan Thomas, Edward's charming mate, is a most gifted sculptor. When it was possible, he escorted John and me into his studio and showed us his recent works of art. The majority of his pieces are different-sized totems. Their sizes were short, medium, and tall. I had to have one! In fact, I wanted to buy two of them. After inquiring on their price, I picked out one tall and one medium size. He said I could pick them up tomorrow if I liked. Perfect!

This summer, also, I will meet Anthony Harvey at a party in the Hamptons. He shared with me his heavy involvement in the theater but failed to tell me to what extent. He did mention that he knew Katharine Hepburn and that his brother was John Standing. John Standing was the brilliant actor who starred opposite Maggie Smith in that production of *Private Lives*, that Deborah and I saw.

After a bit of research, I discover that Anthony was the director in Katharine Hepburn's *The Lion in Winter*. I call Tony and immediately ask him to lunch. He comes clean and confesses his many great achievements. Wow! This man directed my Kate and became the closest of friends. Cool!

1999

LANDMARK CONSERVANCY

John Strangi

The Landmark Conservancy has remained one of my favorite charities through the years. Granted, they never decided to declare me a landmark, but they will learn. One weekend they were having a gala/benefit on *Forbes* yacht, the *Highlander*. That sounds like fun so I booked two tickets for John and me. We boarded the yacht midday. As yachts go, it was nice but not as impressive as I imagined. Once one has been on Ari's yacht, nothing compares. I wish! The *Highlander* has five guest staterooms, six salons, six crew staterooms, and fourteen heads. It was a nice couple of hours sipping champagne and mingling with many familiar faces. I always enjoyed seeing Peg Breen, the Landmark's president. What a charming and lovely woman she is.

John Strangi

After a few hours we were headed back home but, since we were dressed in our Sunday best, decided to stop off at the Plaza's Oak Bar for a cocktail or two. As I looked into the bar, I became totally dumbfounded. The majority of its patrons were dressed in blue jeans and watching a football game on the TV. One dude actually had his feet up on the bar. I could not believe it! The Oak Bar has always been one of New York's best and could easily be classified a landmark. "What the hell is going on!" I felt like I was at TGIF. I know I tend to be a bit dramatic, but I found this so sad. I decided to ask a bartender to summon a manager for me. The manager showed up after about ten minutes. I made him aware of my complaints and he did apologize and proceeded to explain that with the hotel's new ownership, certain rules have changed a bit. He did say, however, he would still share my grievances with the managers. I am not saying that one always has to be in black tie, but some minor dress code might be a plus.

Interestingly enough, about a month later when I was asked to meet friends at the Oak Bar for cocktails, the bar did seem to have their act a bit more together. I must have not been the only one that complained.

Back in the Hamptons, one of my new semi-hobbies was collecting old cars. Every summer the Hamptons are host to a vintage car auction. Did someone say *auction*? One Saturday afternoon I snuck out to it and came home with a beautiful 1956 Lincoln Continental. I paid around $25,000. It was white with a red interior. They were built like trucks back then. It was hardly the most comfortable car to drive, but it was lovely to look at. Maybe I could wire it for a lamp. Since I hardly drove it at all, I would eventually keep it in storage for several years. Every so often, I would take it out for a drive. It was just so damn big!

Years later, I would sell it for practically nothing. A month after I sold it, I heard that there was to be an auction from Elvis Presley's estate. No, I was not hoping on going to it, but his favorite car was auctioned, and this car was an exact replica of my Lincoln Continental. They were identical in every way. To think I had just sold mine for practically nothing! The agony of defeat!

John Strangi

My favorite car, was my 1979 English white Jaguar with red leather interior. I bought it from a fellow who had been driving it around town with a For Sale sign on it. I loved that car. Year by year, though, it appeared to be plagued with problems. One day, flames, all of a sudden, started coming out from under its front hood. This is not a good thing. It was time to say farewell to my Jag. It was a nice five-year run.

I also, this year, became friends with a Joe Pintauro. Joe is a most-celebrated poet, playwright, and author. He owns a charming house in Sag Harbor. Bay Street has premiered many of his plays in their theater. If my writings are even one-tenth as successful as Joe's, I will be satisfied.

It is rumored that a huge celebration for Noel Coward's hundredth birthday was going to be held sometime this year at Carnegie Hall:

Mad About the Boy

One Hundredth Birthday Celebration of the Timeless

Words and Music of Sir Noel Coward

This is one show I simply would have to see! Sir Noel's birthday celebration would be on a single night, naturally, but as soon as tickets become available, I would simply have got to grab one. Noel Coward was such a genius! On December 16, Sir Noel's birthday, this gala evening would blossom at Carnegie Hall.

I waited patiently for ticket sales to begin. The day advertised and I make plans to get in front of Carnegie Hall's ticket booth as soon as possible. I excitedly arrive there a little after twelve. I stand in line looking admiringly at the immense billboard of all the stars, signed to grace this grand event. Among the many are Edward Albee, Elaine Stritch, Barbara Cook, Celeste Holm, Diana Rigg, Bobby Short, Dorothy Loudon, Marian Seldes, and Bobby Short. Wow! What an evening this will be!

It is my turn in the line. I am so excited that my turn, at last, has arrived. Sadly, the ticket lady informs me that the show is sold out. There are no more tickets for sale. I am crushed! What a disappointment! I do not know when I have ever wanted to see a show so much! Damn! Damn! Damn!

The morning of December 16 arrives. I awake, prepare the coffee in my kitchen, and then grab the *New York Times* at my front door. While sitting at my kitchen table, sipping my coffee, and reading the paper, I turn to the entertainment section of the newspaper.

The advertisement for Noel Coward's Gala at Carnegie Hall stands out among all the others. I find this most disturbing. Why could I not have been one of the lucky ones to get tickets for it? It was during my second cup of coffee that an idea hit me. "I will be a part of Noel Coward's gala this evening no matter what! Mark my word!"

I go downstairs, walk over to Park Avenue, and then proceed to a shop that sells art supplies. I purchase several large white pieces of cardboard along with some black markers. I take my art supplies home and begin my Carnegie Hall plot. I place one of the pieces of cardboard on my office desk and proceed to create a large sign. On this sign, I write in large black letters, Noel Coward Fanatic Will Pay Any Price for a Seat at Tonight's Gala! I stand this immense work of art in front of my large bedroom mirror and give it my approval. "Good job, well done!" I will stand in front of Carnegie Hall tonight with this placard and get that ticket for Sir Noel's birthday! I also decide to dress to the hilt and wear my tuxedo. This has got to work!

The evening arrives, so I put on my tux, roll up my placard, and take a cab to Carnegie Hall a few hours before the show is to begin. During the cab ride, I wonder if my plot will succeed or not. Will the staff at Carnegie Hall object to my strange behavior and take me away in handcuffs? Will my bizarre plan make me look like a crazy fool? I do not care! I am going through with it!

I arrive at Carnegie Hall, and even though it is several hours before the show, it seems to be quite busy. There are scads of other people in the same predicament as me trying to get tickets. Only they are not as smart as I am. They do it the old way of just going to the ticket booth and begging. I am this evening *Albert Einstein*, thank you very much!

I inspect the premises, looking for the proper spot to stand with my placard. After about ten minutes, I find the idea spot. I unroll the placard and have at it. Many patrons acknowledge me, and most seem to find my plot amusing. After about thirty minutes, I decide that my striking pose does not seem to be working. I decide to advertise walking from side to side. Thirty minutes later, that does not seem to be working either. I then decide to go inside to the lobby. No, that does not seem to work immediately either. Unsuccessful, an hour later, I give up hope and decide to give in and just stand in the line to the ticket booth like the others. I am still holding my sign, though! It is getting closer and closer to showtime.

As I am standing in line, doing my best to fight off depression, an older gentleman pats me on the back. Oh no, has my deepest fear come true? Could this be Carnegie Hall's manager ready to take me away in handcuffs? Please, no jail! I look lousy in stripes!

Well, happily it was not. This charming man informs me that he does have an extra ticket and that he would sell it to me if I liked. Luckily, he does not take my sign message seriously and asks only for the regular price. I would have paid double! Hell, I would have paid triple! I cannot believe my luck. I am beyond thrilled! I could kiss this fellow!

Our seats are in the front balcony, which is fine. I would sit in the rafters if I had to. We go upstairs. Positive thinking has paid off at last!

The overture begins. Edward Albee is the first to introduce the show. ("My friend, thank you very much.") His speech was superb! Celebrity after celebrity would follow him: Michael Feinstein, Celeste Holm, Barbara Cook, and Bobby Short were among the many. All the music, the dancing, and the singing were all first rate! Elaine Stritch will be the last performance of the evening. She was super! The evening was to last three hours and a half, and unbelievably, it seemed to go by rather quickly. All of that immense talent in one place makes the evening fly by. What a golden evening! I still cannot believe I have seen it! At the evening's close, I, once again, thank the man who gave me the tickets. I told him that he is on my Christmas list for life.

John met me after the show, and we had dinner at a restaurant in Lincoln Center. I remain on cloud nine for the rest of the evening. Where there is a will, there is a way!

MY TEN-THOUSAND-DOLLAR EVENING

It is summer and time for Bay Street Theater's annual benefit gala in Sag Harbor. I have reserved a table for the evening. We have invited Debra, Gloria, and my stockbroker from Washington, Dawn Bennett, as our guests. Another couple, Mark Scwarz, a lawyer from NYC, and his date, a buxom blonde, will also be at our table. Sybil Burton, whom I have grown to love, shows us to our table.

The benefit's auditorium is crawling with celebrities. Bay Street has developed the best of reputations, attracting so many of New York's major stars. Among them this year are Alec Baldwin, Chevy Chase, and to everyone's surprise, Julie Andrews. Beat still, my heart! We spot Julie jumping around from table to table. "I'm over here, Julie!"

At each year's benefit, there is always an exciting auction. Did someone say *auction*? I had read on the flyer that one of the auction items was to have Julie Andrews record a message for your answering machine. Well, this is something I simply had to have. I decide, early on, that I will bid on this to its end no matter what. I shared this decision with no one. I will surprise them!

After a calling of the evening's first auction items, it is time for the *piece de resistance,* my answering machine message. The bidding begins with one thousand dollars made by yours truly. A voice far away from me yells two thousand. Not to be outdone, I yell three thousand, countered by four thousand. I then holler five thousand. It becomes obvious that the bidding will be solely between me and this other fellow. He then yells six thousand. I follow with seven thousand. The crowd is getting excited. Tension is mounting! He then yells eight thousand. You guessed it. I then yelled nine thousand, followed with his ten thousand. I take a deep breath. There is silence for a moment. The auctioneer then asks for ten thousand five hundred. After another deep breath, I bid ten thousand five hundred. He bids eleven thousand. "Let this insane bidding end, for God's sake!" I counter with twelve thousand thinking this will be the end. True to form, he counters with twelve thousand five hundred.

That is it! He wins! I give up and place no more bids. With my head hanged low, I accept defeat. While the champion bidder is basking in his success, two Bay Street employees come to my table and say that Julie would do one for me for ten thousand dollars. I have to give this some thought. That thrill of winning is gone. So what should I do? My stockbroker, Dawn, thinks I should buy it, knowing how much it meant to me. I told them I would let them know of my decision before the night is over.

Next, the master of ceremonies announces for one thousand dollars you could come on the stage and have your picture taken with Julie in a group shot. Well, this I have to do! I am the first one on the stage. Ms. Andrews welcomes me with a kiss and thanks me immediately for buying the answering machine message. Since I did not win, I was literally speechless. Twenty or so people followed me on stage for the picture taking session.

Julie Andrews, Mark Schwarz, John Strangi,
Chevy Chase, Alec Baldwin & Company

Lights, camera, action! The time had come for all to position themselves for their Julie snapshot. I was just about to go back over to Julie and ask if we could stand next to each other when my Kodak moment was shattered. That couple from my table was also on the stage for the group shot and Miss Buxom Blonde threw her arms around me, locking me into my, then, position. Julie ended up being in the far-right corner about five feet from me. We were at least close. Alec Baldwin and Chevy Chase were also in the picture. Mr. Chase would be the picture hog of the evening, positioning himself in the center with outstretched arms. A ham is a ham is a ham!

At the evening's close, I whispered to Emma that I would buy the answering machine message for the ten thousand. Bay Street Theater is an outstanding organization, and I am proud to support them.

A few days later during my acting class with Emma, I wrote down what I would like Julie to say on my message. I first told her that I would like Julie to record *two* messages for me. Emma seemed a bit taken aback at my request for *two*, but for ten thousand dollars, I thought I could bend the rules a bit. I would like one message to be for both John and I for our home phone number and the second to be for my "acting phone number." For our home message, I requested her to say, *"Hello, Julie Andrews here. My good friends John and John can't come to the phone right now, but if you'd leave your name and number at the sound of the beep, I'm sure they'll love getting back to you, and always remember, just a spoonful of sugar helps the medicine go down. Bye."* For my private one I merely requested a standard greeting having her say, *"Hello, Julie Andrews here. My good friend John Strangi can't come to the phone right now, but if you'd leave your name and number at the sound of the beep, I'm sure he will love getting back to you. Have a lovely day."*

One weekend Emma would give my instructions to her husband, Stephen, to take over to Julie to record them. Stephen does so, and a week later Emma presents me with my recording. Excitedly, I take the tape home to listen to it. I go into my library where I can savor my golden moment in peace. I place the tape in my recorder and listen. The recording for John and I is fine. It is the one for just me where there is a problem. Ms. A. pronounces my name wrong. She pronounces "Strangi" with a strong *G* instead of a soft *G*. I have no choice but to ask Emma to have her make another recording for me. I shyly ask Emma at our next meeting. Julie makes a new recording the following week, pronouncing my name correctly. To think that years after I played Henry Higgins I would one day be giving the original Eliza Dolittle voice lessons. Is this cool or what?

I have decided to sell the house in the Hamptons. The Hamptons has turned into a bit of a chore. Two of our friends in the Hamptons are real estate brokers. I call them and tell them I would like to list my place with them. They are thrilled to get my business and list my house immediately. I am hoping that with their real estate magic they will be able to unload my house in record time. Oh please! Oh please! Oh please!

"Nobody knows the trouble I've seen, nobody knows but me." One month goes by with no sale, followed by two months, and then three months. You can guess where this is going. Ten months goes by and there is no sale. I am most unpleased. I am not a happy camper. I am not asking for miracles. Well, maybe I am. I just want my house sold!

Since I have not worked for a while, I thought maybe I would try my hand at day trading. After all, I did work on Wall Street for almost fifteen years. Maybe a little luck would come my way. I begin examining the trusty *Wall Street Journal* daily. I begin investing a little money in this and a little money in that. Actually, I invested a little too much money in that. Buy! Sell! Buy! Sell! I am doing okay, but I am no Rockefeller. After a few months of minor success, I decide to go a different route.

I decide to look for a job. That was that nine-to-five thing I once had. How did that work? I look in the *New York Times* and go job hunting. I apply with a nearby agency. They send me out on several interviews. After a few unsuccessful tries, I am off to an interview on Forty-Seventh Street in the fashion district. This particular House of Fashion was looking for help in their data processing department. I am to start immediately. My job will be in front of a computer in a rather large office/room with about seven other workers. They all seemed harmless. My supervisor was a woman in her early forties. She seemed sweet and easy to work with. It was her boss, the company's main honcho, who gave me mixed feelings. Let's call him Bob, only to protect the guilty. I just had bad feelings about him from day one. Every cloud has a silver lining. Unfortunately, my cloud also contained a tornado.

I make it to my fourth week, and on a rather slow day, I decide, when few of my coworkers were not around to look at my personal stock portfolio on my computer. I know that this is a no-no, but one must live dangerously. I go into the required Web site, and just as my portfolio takes over my computer's screen, our infamous Bob walks into the room. He sees what I have on my computer screen. He is not pleased. I am instantly fired. How dare I do such a thing on company time!

In all fairness, I was totally in the wrong. I should not have done what I did. I take full blame. It was stupid of me to do such a thing at work. It is "Bye, bye, Fashion Industry!" I never wanted to be another Ralph Lauren anyway.

Getting back to the Hamptons situation, nothing seems to be happening with my real estate friends. They are not moving my house at all. After nine months, I give my house listing to another real estate broker to handle. My now ex-friends are not happy that I took my listing away from them. That is just too bad! I am sorry, but I gave them plenty of time!

Oh, and guess what I found at the end of the year. There is a wonderful memorabilia shop located just down the street from us on Fifty-Seventh Street called Gotta Have It. Needless to say, I have always walked by their shop and eyed a few things. They had something I simply had to have. I purchased a framed picture and contract of Lucy and Desi with an original ticket to the *I Love Lucy* show. I loved having that ticket! I had never seen one before. It is so cool. It only cost $2,706.25. I love it! Life is good.

Then on top of this, I was able to buy an original Donald Brooks costume design for Julie Andrews from *Star*. Remember I had said Donald promised to give me one of those designs, but never did. Well, I have my design at last. It is so cool. In the movie, she wears this gorgeous red gown at the beginning of a restaurant scene. I purchased it from Profiles in History for $1,677. I love this picture! It is gorgeous!

2001

TOMORROW

I will be turning forty-eight years old, this year. Ouch! I am older than I ever intended to be. However, I am in good shape and I can still run a mile and still make a mean vodka martini.

I begin this year with hopes of tackling a new job. I will become a bartender! Oh, yes! That is the perfect job for me. There are so many outstanding bars in NYC! I love being around people, and no one can make a better dry martini like yours truly! I will be the best! This has to be a fit!

I check the papers and discover a bartender's school downtown on West Thirty-Ninth Street. I really do not think I need to go to one. No one has had more practice of making drinks than me. What is the big deal? I can make a whiskey sour with my eyes closed. Maybe I have to have a license, though. Whatever. I call the school and arrange to start lessons on Tuesday of next week.

I have a choice of a one-week course or a two-week course. I choose the one week, which is Monday to Friday, eight hours a day. One learns the basics, from how to pour a proper ounce to how to shake. You are given a booklet with a million different drinks to study, 99 percent of them never ordered.

I had never seen so many drinks my entire life. "We have to learn all of these?" We do not really have to learn all of them but just be familiar with as many as possible.

Our classroom reminds me somewhat of a theater in the round. It is a semicircle of connected desks with our instructor/bartender in the middle. There are around twenty people in my class, and most of them younger than I. Ouch!

I tried to absorb as much as possible during my 40-hour run, and I thought I was doing rather well. That is, until it came to our final day of class, which was a written test, followed by a "twenty drinks in less than six minutes" test. Forgive me, world, but I am just not a rush, rush kind of a guy. I prefer doing things calmly and methodically. When it was my turn, I approached the bar, grabbed my first bottle, and began my marathon. After making one drink, I became all thumbs, looked up at my classmates, and muttered, "This isn't going to work," and left the classroom. Alas, I have failed again.

"What do I want to be when I grow up?"

Today is my birthday. I have purchased tickets for John and me to see *The Producers* on September 9, 2001, followed by dinner reservations at Sardi's. We had heard so many outstanding reviews on the show and could not wait to see it. For our evening's show, however, an understudy will play Mathew Broderick's role. That is no big deal. At least we still get to see Nathan Lane. We arrive at the theater around seven thirty. We take our center orchestra seats around eight. The overture begins, followed by my standard chills. The first act was good, but we were both unimpressed by the show's immense playing of slapstick. The acting, choreography, and singing were all the best, but neither of us were experiencing the expected glow that the many newspaper ads had promised. The second act was more of the same. Mathew Broderick's understudy could not have been better, but in our eyes, the overall show just did not pan out.

Sardi's was busy as usual. We decided to begin with a few drinks at the upstairs bar. My favorite bartender attends bar upstairs. In the middle of our second drink, a young fellow joins us at the bar. He looks familiar. He turns out to be Mathew Broderick's understudy, whom we had just seen. We, naturally, to him, raved about the show and his performance. We thespians have to stick together. He was very nice. I love hearing of anyone getting his or her big break in the theater. It must be frustrating standing around night after night hoping to go on stage. However, it is all part of the game, and to be an understudy for such a tremendous part is indeed a feather in one's cap.

It was a nice evening all in all. May my forty-eighth year be a good one!

144

SEPTEMBER 11, 2001

It is a beautiful September morning. I wake up early and after my usual two cups of coffee, I shave, shower, and head to my gym to run my five miles. My gym is about five short blocks down Second Avenue. I open its front door and proceed to sign my name at the reception's desk. As I am signing, a fellow runs up to the desk and yells, "Did you hear that a plane just ran into the World Trade Center?" The receptionist says no, she hadn't. He says, "Well, one just did." Not knowing any of the details, we are all thinking the plane was probably some little propeller plane or such.

I head down to the locker room to change amid all this talk of this plane incident. Still not thinking that this plane thing was anything of great proportion, I put on my running shorts, head for a treadmill, and have at it. As in all gyms, television sets hover above in eyes distance. The day's regular broadcasting is interrupted. All of a sudden, the TV shows a shot of the plane that crashed into the side of the World Trade Center. We soon realize that this plane was more than just a little plane. This was a regular passenger jet.

How could this have happened? I as well as everyone around me am in a state of shock and disbelief. I stop my running and decide its best I get home as soon as possible. I do not even change clothes. I just throw my garb into my gym bag and run home. What the hell is going on?

I arrive home. John is in a panic. We do our best to comfort each other. We both become transfixed on our television set. We just cannot believe what we are seeing. Everything is so unreal. How could something like this have happened? Gradually the facts of this horrible event will emerge. At 8:48 a.m. American Airlines Flight 11, a Boeing 767 from Logan International Airport in Boston, carrying eighty-one passengers, will strike One World Trade Center. It now becomes clear that this was no accident.

At 9:00 a.m., John's eyes are still transfixed on the television set. I am nervously pacing from the kitchen to the bedroom where two television set's are located. We are both in a state of shock. What is going to happen next? That downtown area was where we lived and where I worked for so many years. John still has relatives living near that vicinity. Then the unthinkable happens.

At 9:06 a.m., a second plane crashes into Two World Trade Center. Our beautiful city is under attack. We soon learn that this plane was United Flight 175, another Boeing 767, carrying fifty-six passengers. Our twin towers are hit! This is all just too much to believe! How will all of the many people working in those towers escape? This is worse than a nightmare. How can this be happening? Who is responsible for this madness? The flames on each tower seem to be growing and growing! How will the people on those high floors ever escape? Trapped individuals, with no choice, even begin jumping from the windows. It appears that the discarded jet fuel was causing the floors to pancake to the next.

We do not believe our eyes! In just a matter of seconds, the south tower has totally fallen with smoke and fallen debris deposited everywhere. Lower Manhattan looks like a combat zone. How many people left on the tower before its crumbling? How many were able to escape? All, with no other choice, were fleeing frantically on foot. The sky was completely black with smoke.

In less than an hour at 10:28 a.m., the north tower will also crumble to the ground. Our World Trade Center has vanished in seconds. How many people were able to escape? The firefighters are arriving in swarms and doing everything in their power to try to come to everyone's rescue. Everywhere, people are clinging for their lives. As the hours accumulate, sadly, things appear more and more hopeless.

It is war! We now learn that a Flight 77, a Boeing 757 with fifty-eight passengers from Washington's Dulles International Airport, headed for Los Angeles, is hijacked by five, and at 9:37 a.m. crashes into the western side of Washington's Pentagon. All passengers and crew are killed as well as 125 Pentagon personnel.

Flight 93 will be the next victim. As they receive a warning message of the World Trade Center catastrophe, hijackers will storm its cockpit and take over the flight, changing its course to eastward, heading back to Washington. Will the Capitol or the White House be the next targets? At 9:57 a.m., passengers, fully aware of the hijackers' intent, will revolt and decide to do everything in their power to stop these maniacs. Todd Beamer along with other passengers will decide to storm the hijackers and prevent and disrupt them from carrying out their intended mission. Todd Beamer yells, "Are you guys ready? Okay, let's roll!" And roll they did.

At 10:03 a.m. Flight 93 will be crashed by its passengers and hijackers due to the fighting in the cockpit eighty miles southeast of Pittsburgh in Somerset County, Pennsylvania. Todd Beamer and his brave fellow passengers would save our White House and Capitol from being the next victims.

All air traffic is halted. The United States is at a standstill. We soon learn that Osama bin Laden is behind these attacks. These hijackers were trained pilots with the sole pursuit of causing complete chaos. Every hour brings us more disturbing news. The magnitude of deaths reported appears to be without end. Even though we live uptown, blocks and blocks from the tragedy, we still see smoke hovering from downtown. The disturbing smell from the masses of burning debris will hang on for days and weeks.

John and I are both in a total daze. It is all too much to take in. It is hard describing ourselves the next couple of days. It is as if we were robots only functioning because there was no other choice. Our friends, who live outside of New York, call us to make sure we are okay. I did not want Mother to be aware of it. She had not been doing too well this past year, so I wanted this tragedy kept from her. This catastrophe will be with us for a very long time.

We would not go out to dinner for an entire week. When we finally do, it was very strange. After what had happened to those hundreds of innocent people, we felt guilty, somehow, trying to enjoy ourselves even for a second. Wherever we would go in the coming weeks, we would always run into someone who knew someone directly affected by the tragedy. Everywhere, on avenue after avenue, there were pictures posted of missing loved ones. Sadly, they will remain posted for months to come.

I have always said that New Yorkers are tough. We can withstand anything and everything. At least we do our best.

Life must go on.

SEPTEMBER 27, 2001

I had read that Rue McClannahan was going to be starring in a production of *The Women* on Broadway. I had always admired her so very much! From *Maude* to *The Golden Girls* she more than showed the world what a talented lady she is. I definitely planned to get tickets for it.

On September 27, after my daily workout at my gym, I was walking up Second Avenue, home, when I glance at this attractive woman crossing Fifty-Eighth Street. She looks like Rue McClannahan, but I am not sure. I hurriedly inch my way next to her. We are then standing next to each other waiting for the traffic light to change. I look at her. She looks at me. I look at her. She looks at me. I want to say something, but it is her nose that gives me pause. She does not have one. I mean it is a Nannette Fabray–type nose. It is so faint that it makes me doubt that it is really her and I do not say anything.

I go up to my apartment, sick that I did not tell her how much I love and admire her. It had to have been her! What to do? What to do? I know! I will write her a letter and send it to the American Airlines Theater where *The Women* will be playing. I decide to compose the letter in the style of Sophia in *The Golden Girls*: *Picture it. New York City, September 2001*

I mail the letter, and a week later, much to my surprise, I receive a handwritten letter from her with and autographed picture. She was touched by my letter, and she would like me to come backstage to see her after her one of her performances of *The Women*.

I purchase tickets immediately for John and I. *The Women* was always one of my favorite movies. We could not wait to see it! Unfortunately, we did not think this production of it was very well done. With the exception of Rue's part, as the Countess, we just did not think it worked. We did get to meet with Rue after the show and walk her to a cab. We kissed. She was charming!

Speaking of charming, it is time for a Julie fix. Back in the Hamptons, on November 11, Bay Street Theater is having a benefit gala honoring Julie Andrews. It will be a one-woman show chronicling her career. With the many highlights of Ms. Andrews's immense theatrical career on a movie screen behind her, she will spend close to two hours discussing her magical life. With show tickets, one can also purchase tickets for attending dinner with her after at the American Hotel. I buy the whole bundle.

It was a Saturday evening's show. John and I arrived at the theater around seven thirty. The wonderful Sybil Burton will greet us at the door and always with a kiss. We exchange greetings with Emma and Stephen as well. We see many of our Hampton friends there. The curtain went up at eight and Julie looked radiant. With TV and movie clippings flashing behind her, she took us on a glorious journey through her career. Every second was golden.

After the show, we proceeded to the American Hotel to dine with our Mary Poppins. Luckily, our little table was not too far from Julie's. She had a rather large table for her and her entourage which, naturally, included Emma, Stephen, and Sybil. I had not seen Emma for about a month and thought she looked particularly lovely this evening. She had lost weight and looked quite striking. So just before dessert, I went over to Emma, who was seated directly opposite from Julie, and said, "Va va va voom, Emma, you look fantastic!" Then Julie all of a sudden summoned me to her side with a kiss. She thanked me for the red roses presented to her at the beginning of her show. She had assumed that I had given them to her. Does this Dame know I am her biggest fan or what? I then replied,

"You're welcome." The thing is I had not sent her those roses. Go with the flow.

What a lovely evening. This will mark my third Julie kiss.

2002

MONEY MAKES THE WORLD GO ROUND

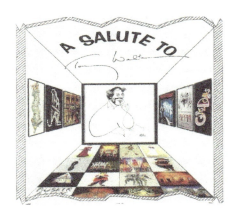

January 21 marked a special day on our calendar. A gala honoring Tony Walton was being held at the Russian Tea Room. Tony was, of course, Julie Andrews's first husband and is Emma's father. What a major talent that man is! His many awards for his costume and scenic design are endless.

It was a lovely evening with many a celebrity there to honor Tony. Elaine May and Mike Nichols began the evening with a classic performance. I spoke with Susan Strohman, who I had not seen for a while. Nathan Lane was there. It was great to meet him. What a talent! Julie was there, of course, looking as lovely as ever. This will mark our fourth kiss.

One thing I must praise Tony for is his extreme modesty. It was during one of Bay Street's benefit galas when John and I spoke with Tony for a while. John told him of his twenty-two years working in window display at Lord & Taylor. Tony could not have been more complimentary to John, throwing more and more praise his way. This genius was making John feel his accomplishments were equally important as his own. What a giant of a man!

It does not make much of a dent in my bank account, but I did obtain more acting jobs this year than many others. Who would have thought that my "more mature" look would land me more jobs?

I took my picture and resume to an agency that was known for their massive work for extras.

One of my first assignments was with the television show *Law & Order*. It is filmed at one of their studios located in the Chelsea Pier. (*Matt Lauer fame.*) I would do sixteen episodes spread out during a number of months. My role will be that of lawyer/press reporter most of the time. My exposure on each would vary from episode to episode. I always admired Sam Waterston, one of its regulars, and got to meet him during one of our lunch breaks. Just as he was biting into a salami sandwich, I told him that I have admired his talents ever since I saw him in *The Glass Menagerie* with Katharine Hepburn. I also met Jerry Orbach who was charming.

Ed was my next TV assignment. I was on six episodes of it. Its shooting location was outside of the city, so we extras went by bus. Most of the shooting was at a bowling alley. It was a lot of fun, but I believe I had less exposure on this one.

Oz was next on the list. I played an execution spectator. The majority of their shots were from a jailhouse. During one of its episodes, Rita Moreno, who had a guest spot in the show often, was seated directly in front of me. She introduced herself to us. She was charming. I wish I had told her that we had mutual friends. My good friend, Stanley Hura, has been one of her closest friends for years. I must learn how to name-drop.

I was lucky enough to work in a few movies as well. *Maid in Manhattan*, starring Jennifer Lopez, was the first of the films I was to work on. I reported to a room where there were probably about seventy extras waiting for their orders. The woman in charge asked, "If any of you fellows can lead a lady on the dance floor, raise your hand." Thinking that it is the dancers who would be getting the best exposure on this film, I raise my hand. So what if I can't dance. I am the first to admit that I have two left feet. I am assigned to be one of the dancers. Pity the girl assigned to being my dancing partner. One must pity her feet anyway. I tell my friends I landed the part of a dancer and they are all hysterical. They are all aware of my Fred Astaire talents.

The scene is filmed in the Metropolitan Art Museum. Special permission had to be granted with shooting around such priceless artifacts. One of our first instructions was not to touch anything. If anyone does, we are out of there. It was exciting to be surrounded by so many priceless artifacts. We men dancers must dress in black tie, naturally. The men were asked to stand on one side of the immense room and the women on the other. We were the paired-off boy-girl boy-girl. God pity the poor woman whom I was assigned to. All of the dancers are asked to wear little plastic bags over their shoes to keep the microphones from picking up the clicking of our dance shoes.

My partner was a lovely woman probably about the same age as me. She was dressed in a very glittery silver gown. She soon became aware of my lack of talent on the dance floor but was cool about it. I did okay with the exception of stepping on her toes, one or two hundred times. Seriously, I was okay. I will refer to her as Mitzi, to protect the guilty.

Our scene is that of when Jennifer Lopez, Marisa Ventura, is to meet Ralph Fiennes, Christopher Marshall, at a benefit at the Met. Marisa, unbeknownst to Christopher, is a housekeeper at the Waldorf Astoria. For this benefit, though, she manages to look like a princess. She is gorgeous! Stanley Tucci and Natasha Richardson will also be in the scene. I have admired Mr. Tucci's work for years, as well as Ms. Richardson's.

I was a bit turned off by the diva treatment Ms. Lopez seemed to be requesting. I suppose when one is collecting twenty million dollars for a picture, certain demands are to be expected. Between takes, she relaxed in a large leather easy chair with a girl on each side fanning her. Maybe I was just jealous. Why the hell aren't they fanning me?

One, two, three and. One, two, three and. One, two, three and. One, two, three and. I was feeling just like the king in *The King and I*. For four days Mitzi and I would be waltzing nonstop. I do not know how Fred and Ginger stood it for all of those years. However, I survived as well as Mitzi.

When the movie came out, I would say I have about seven seconds of exposure. One can see me for a few seconds immediately after Jennifer and Ralph meet, and I am in a few other very quick shot's after. I danced for four days straight for seven seconds of exposure! "What I did for love."

Birth, starring Nicole Kidman, was my next movie. It took place in a movie theater outside of the city. It, too, involved a bus ride. I wore a suit playing the part of an audience member. It was a day's shoot. Nicole looked quite lovely. I was most pleased with the amount of time the camera stayed focused on me this time out. It was a good ten to fifteen seconds. That is like winning the lottery coming from an extra. I did not think *Birth* was one of Nicole's best, but every movie cannot be a *Gone with the Wind*, I guess.

Next on my movie list was *Anger Management,* starring Jack Nicholson. I was one of two thousand extras. The scene shoots at Yankee Stadium. I was going to take the subway to the shoot but decided to take a cab instead. You see what moving uptown does to you. My agent asked me to wear a blue sport coat to the shoot. No problem, I have the perfect outfit for it. I arrive at the shoot and am then told to just go up and sit anywhere on the bleachers. The casting agent will assign us to our proposed seat after.

Some of us also become aware that for this scene Mayor Giuliani and his girlfriend will be having a guest spot. Several hours pass when I see the mayor and girlfriend arrive. I am high up in the bleachers where they are below, but still in the same vicinity. All of a sudden, the director yells to me to come down from the higher bleachers. He then requests me to sit about five rows closer to the mayor. After about an hour, I have the surprise of my life. The director informs me that he wants me to sit in the front row next to the mayor, his girlfriend, and the movie's two producers. I shook Mayor Giulianni's hand and thanked him for his monumental help after 9/11. They then direct me to an area on the side for hair and makeup. I cannot believe that this is happening. Out of all these hundreds of extras, they pick me for this key role. At last, it appears I will be discovered. "Move over, Brad Pitt! So long, Matt Damon. Strangi has arrived!"

We shoot for about four hours. It was all so exciting! Take after take after take. How I love every minute. With all this footage taken of me, you know I'll be seen. I just have to be! The shoot ends and I say my good-byes. I take a cab home but after this breathtaking experience feel like I could have flown. I am on cloud nine!

Thoroughly Modern Millie will win best musical this year along with its stars Sutton Foster winning best actress and Harriett Harris winning best supporting. It was a brilliant musical, and the new songs added to it are all topnotch. The choreography is outstanding as well. I saw it several times.

Elaine Stritch at Liberty was the other big hit of the season. It is brilliant. Ms. Stritch takes you on a journey through her entire life, beginning with her childhood in Detroit and then on to her outstanding New York theatrical career. John and I will go see it twice. During the show she kiddingly comments that she has the best acceptance speech prepared for a Tony and has had it for forty-five years. Well, I am thrilled to say she was able to use her acceptance for this masterpiece.

Ms. Stritch is such a talented woman! I am sorry I never saw her in *Company*, but I still did see her in several other Broadway shows.

MEMORIES LIGHT THE CORNERS
OF MY MIND

What can I say? I bought when I should have sold. I sold when I should have bought.

I put my trust in those who were undeserving.

Let's leave it at that.

I really had thought that I would be living in New York City my entire life, but thanks to my madcap behavior and bizarre money management, that dream will be shattered before the end of this year. The year began with me still getting my share of acting work in movies and TV.

My first job was as an extra in Mike Nichols's TV movie *Angels in America*. I worked on it for several days and in several different scenes. In the movie's very flamboyant funeral scene, I am one of the pallbearers. I can be seen for about two seconds. Just do not blink! It was exciting getting to see Mike Nichols work his magic. He is such a genius!

I then had a walk on in *How to Lose a Guy in Ten Days*, starring Kate Hudson and Matthew McConaughey. It involved a couple of days' shoot. Kate Hudson is a cutie!

Mona Lisa Smile, starring Julia Roberts, was next. I sat in a church pew for hours and hours. Ms. Roberts was only a few rows from me, but I ended up with no exposure in this one at all.

Anger Management had its premiere. I could not wait to see it! My moment of triumph is just around the corner! The second the movie came out in local theaters, I grabbed a seat. Scene by scene I waited patiently for my big moment. The scene at Yankee Stadium arrives at last. You first see a single shot of Mayor Giuliani followed by a single shot of his girlfriend. Then both producers have their moment in the spotlight. There was no shot of me. Once again, my fame tossed on the cutting room floor! Rejection! Rejection! Rejection!

During one month when I was quite busy with extra work, I unfortunately missed one of my calls. It was *Saturday Night Live* calling to ask me to appear in that Saturday's show. I did not retrieve their message till late Saturday evening. I was sick that I missed that call! I would have loved to have appeared on that show. It has been on the air almost the entire time that I have lived in New York. If you happen to be reading this, *SNL*, "I'm ready for my close-up!"

My house in East Hampton does sell early in the year. That was a relief, but it really did not help much in the money management department. It was just one less bill to pay each month. I never should have bought that house with a mortgage. I had more than enough money then to buy it out right. Should have! Would have! Could have!

I was counting on some land I own in Texas to sell as well as a half a dozen of natural gas wells to be built but nothing has come of it.

It pains me to say it, but it looks like I will have to sell our Fifty-Ninth Street apartment. We find a real estate agent and have it listed. Finding a buyer takes longer than I anticipated, but after about six months, a buyer does materialize. With the sale, I will be more than tripling my investment, but the money really does not make me feel better about the prospect of moving.

John had always hoped that we might one day move to Florida. It looks like his dream will be coming true. We had vacationed in Fort Lauderdale and Sarasota before, but we decide on Palm Beach being our new residence. We fly out there and find a very nice two-bedroom apartment overlooking the intercostal in West Palm Beach. Our moving day is Friday the thirteenth! June 13, 2003. I think that date says it all.

I will miss Manhattan like crazy! What an adjustment to make after thirty long years! I do not know how I will ever adjust to living outside of the city. My dreams of making it in the theater never came true, but somehow, simply being a resident of Manhattan made me feel like a star. Even with the millions of people living there, I still got the feeling that we were all one big family. No other city in the world can bring out such feelings.

I know that this must sound extremely ungrateful, but I sometimes wish I had never been given that ticket to "Easy Street." Seriously, when I was just making ends meet, my first twenty years, I made things work out, and I was damn proud of myself for it. I made my New York dream come true.

To all of you actors out there I can only say *never give up*. That dream may never come true, but you can create a damn exciting life trying for it. New Yorkers are a species unto themselves, and I mean that as the highest praise. Possibly one has to be an actor for one to identify with the magic one feels in the theater.

We actors merely live from day to day, but all come alive when that curtain goes up.

Always remember, "You are as good as the best that you ever were!"

THERE'S NO BUSINESS LIKE SHOW BUSINESS

JOHN STRANGI'S TEN COMMACTMENTS

1. Learn to cook.
2. Find something positive in all rejections.
3. Replace martinis with iced tea.
4. Project and play to that balcony.
5. Marry an accountant.
6. Sleep with that director.
7. Stay away from the golf clubs. Try stamp collecting.
8. Stand clear of all auction houses.
9. If lucky enough to obtain residence in NYC, keep it for life!
10. If you are not a success in show business, write a book!

SEPTEMBER 1972

FAIRY TALES CAN COME TRUE, THEY CAN HAPPEN TO YOU

Well, my lifelong dream has finally come true. I am moving to New York City to be an actor. I cannot believe that the day has finally come. I have waited so long for this dream to become reality.

I could barely sleep last night, with all the anticipation of the next day's events. I have a nine o'clock flight in the morning. All my loved ones are with me at the airport to wish me good-bye. It's an emotional moment, but I am too excited to be anything but happy and exuberant. After many kisses and hugs, I am off.

The flight gets off to a nice start. I asked for a window seat where I could have a first-hand look at the grand New York City skyline when we land.

I am still bubbling with excitement. I just cannot believe it! Lunchtime arrives and I ask the flight attendant for a cocktail in celebration. I decide on ordering a drink. Wait! Hold it! Something is not right here. John Strangi wants to be an actor? Shy, introverted Johnny? This just cannot be for real!

If I could only do it all over again.

ABOUT THE AUTHOR

It was in 1964, John Strangi, age eleven, was to visit New York City for the first time. His Father, Albert, would treat him to an entire week in the Big Apple, taking him to the New York Worlds Fair. He was to fall in love with the City instantly and swore to himself that he would one day make New York City his home. Its magic energy would totally captivate him.

The first Broadway show he would see would be in 1967 when he and his brother Albert were in NYC for a few days. They would see *Hello Dolly* starring Betty Grable. The evening was magical! The magic he felt in NYC three years earlier is as strong as ever.

His love for the theater came alive in high school. The smell of grease paint would capture him, landing him roles in *The King And I*, *Wait Until Dark*, *Plaza Suite*, and *My Fair Lady*. Starring as Henry Higgins in *My Fair Lady* was a dream come true.

In New York City, he will study acting at the American Academy of Dramatic Arts, the HB Studio in Greenwich Village, and from Emma Walton and Stephen Hamilton at the Bay Street Theater in Sag Harbor.

His dream of making it on Broadway was not to be, but he did work quite a bit in television and movies making him a lifelong member of SAG/AFTRA.

Simply living day to day in New York City, made John feel like a star.

CPSIA information can be obtained
at www.ICGtesting.com
Printed in the USA
LVOW05s1032240317
528375LV00023B/258/P